"Readers are in for an authentic description of a seven year old's journey from Communist Hungary to the United States of America. The danger, excitement, courage and gratitude contained in the author's family memories are a credit to our mutual human spirit. Knowing the storyteller as I do, America is also a better place thanks to his struggle and achievement."

~ **Chris Lauzen,** Illinois State Senator 1993-2012

Kane Country Board Chairman 2013-2016

"Those who cannot remember the past are condemned to repeat it."

~ George Santayana

FROM TYRANNY TO LIBERTY

A PERSONAL STORY

Béla (Bill) Suhayda

JONES MEDIA
PUBLISHING

PUBLISHED BY:
Jones Media Publishing
YourBookBlueprint.com

ISBN: 978-0-9973408-4-6 paperback
Second Edition 2020

DEDICATION

To my parents,
Irén Menrath Suhayda and Lajos Z. Suhayda,
who brought their family halfway around the world to live as
free people, and to all the freedom fighters, Ishpeming Michigan
Rotarians, Hungarians, Austrians and Americans who made our
journey and assimilation in the U.S. possible.

CONTENTS

FOREWORD

Freedom isn't free. It isn't free to protect, nor is it free to achieve. There is sacrifice involved in both

A family's struggle for liberty, in this true story, starts in the hearts of the parents of three young boys. The parents fear that the totalitarian communist regime that has already extinguished personal freedoms in their native country will stop at nothing to preserve their idea of national order. Imagine a parent's choice: throw away everything your family has, and risk even your children's lives to opt for liberty, or settle for a life of tyranny dictated by fear.

Personal liberty has become a natural part of American history and culture going back to our very beginnings. We celebrate it as we are mindful of the men and women who fought and died to preserve it. We often look to the deeds, writings and memories of our founding fathers and American service men to keep its spirit burning in our hearts.

The story you are about to experience deals with the events of a courageous family as they navigate past Secret Service agents and across a border that is both mined and guarded by snipers who have orders to shoot to kill anyone attempting to cross it. Through the eyes of a young boy, you the reader will meet real-life heroes as they assist in this family's journey while risking greatly to help in their escape.

There are and always will be threats to our liberty. Today's world is under assault from international terrorist organizations, bloated government bureaucracies, and associated corruption. Our country is also experiencing an erosion of our personal rights along with creeping socialism. A critical first step in protecting our freedom is being reminded of its cost and what life would be without it.

To sustain our spirit of liberty, the stories of those who risked everything to possess it must be told and preserved. For this reason, those who love freedom owe a tremendous debt of gratitude to this courageous family you are about to meet in this compelling story.

Keith R. Wheeler
State Representative
50th District, Illinois

PREFACE

Pancakes and Liberty

Have you ever watched pancakes being made? The batter mixture flows smoothly and evenly in circular patterns on the griddle until they cook into delicious round breakfast wafers. Hmmmm....I must be hungry. Isn't it interesting, though, that the shape of each is never square or triangular? Amazingly, they are almost always uniformly circular in shape. Well, maybe it isn't all that amazing. I found myself considering this idea this morning. I laid in bed, with my pancake making wife, Brenda, asleep next to me and thought about the forces at play that have kept every pancake round since the beginning of pancake pouring history. Gravity and fluid dynamics make for delicious flat discs every time. These same two forces have also organized the universe into billions and billions of spherical glowing masses of stars and planets all spinning and moving in circular patterns. Nature is easy to figure out, and even predictable, if we understand her laws.

I love nature, so maybe why I became a biology/science teacher isn't as big of a mystery as why pancakes are round. The reason my parents, along with tens of thousands of other Hungarian families, decided to risk everything to take their children and flee an abusive communist regime there in '56 was no mystery to the world either. Self-determination is a strong force of the human spirit and most people in our world understand that. So it is somewhat amazing to me that we have so many people in our society who think nothing of giving it away. A person with freedom is a person with choices. Wanting your children to have their own choices, for reaching their full potential, is also a dream most parents have. These emotions are as natural, in human experience, as gravity or even fluid dynamics is in nature.

So it is curious to me that we have as many people in the world settling for dependence. And this has become a very unnatural trend in our country today. Close to half of our citizens here in the U.S. rely on some form of government assistance. Fifty years ago, only five percent of our citizens had that kind of dependence. And we have Bernie Sanders, a self admitted socialist with huge support from the youth of America, running for the presidency. We are at a tipping point! Have we become corrupted as a people? Has the welfare state along with all of our other social programs disincentivized a work ethic in our citizens?

Producing dependence in communist countries is accomplished in a different way. It is done through the application of brute force. Big Government control and ownership over every aspect of a country's economics creates half of that dependence. This control starts with nationalizing all wealth and property including all land ownership. The stripping away of personal liberties from citizens makes up the other half. Perfect equity (everyone makes the same wage) among the citizenry of a country, which is communism's ultimate aim, cannot be achieved in any other way than through force. Communists have to mold their citizens into pliable, selfless, Eloi [1] in order to make their system work. Those citizens

---

1 In H.G. Wells fiction novel, The Time Machine, there is a society of child-like adults who have been educated to not have a purpose, curiosity, or discipline. They live in an environment in which strength and intellect are no longer used, and are not seen as important to survival. These are the perfect characteristics of people under communism. And this is what happens to people when big brother takes over their lives. George Orwell wrote two books
(cont. on next page.)

resisting this "reeducation" are culled from the population. They simply "disappear." I think every one of our Universities should offer at least one class concerning the genocides that have been perpetrated by governments against their people. However, I hesitate to suggest that they should be mandated to take such a course. I value individual freedom too much to do that.

Human civilizations have teetered between chaotic wilderness existences, with no laws, to tyrannical totalitarian regimes that have enslaved and even murdered millions of their populations. (Google Stalin and the Ukraine for details). I think almost everyone believes in freedom for themselves, but they don't necessarily believe in freedom for others. We will always have people in our society, and in government, who decide that they know better than the rest of us how we should live. The founders of this country understood that. So they produced a Constitution (a set of "rules") for those who govern us now and who have governed this nation throughout its history. The Constitution of the United States has kept our government in check and our people protected from the despots who would rule over them. The Constitution has worked to limit the powers of government. Many of those "rules" are being ignored and trampled in recent times. Our constitution is under siege today. We had better understand that America's greatness comes from our concept of the importance of LIBERTY. It is this freedom that has allowed our people to be more creative and, as a result, more prosperous than every other country on the planet. America is great because of an idea.

People who have been denied their natural God-given rights to liberty, and who suffered under dictatorships, have fled those totalitarian states flocking to the U.S. in droves. They, better than even the American people, understood the fundamental importance of individual and economic

---

that all Americans should read. They are "1984 and "Animal Farm." These books depict what happens to people under repressive regimes. I doubt there are more than a handful of University professors in our country today who have these books as mandatory reading. I sincerely hope that I'm wrong. I'm sure that they have quite a large selection of books to be read by Karl Marx including "The Communist Manifesto."

freedoms. That is why people have come here from communist countries all over the world including Eastern Europe and Cuba. They are searching for liberty and the prosperity it creates in a free enterprise system.

My family's story, which I have attempted to put into print here, is not unlike millions of other stories of people looking to escape oppression in exchange for opportunity and individual liberty. It is unique only in its personal detail. It has been the great fortune of my family to succeed in finding our equity in opportunity by coming to the U.S. There were many others who were not as fortunate as we were. Many forfeited their lives in the effort. The personal story I relate here is just one in thousands of other scenarios of Hungarians who succeeded in escaping communism during and after the Revolution of '56. We are very fortunate to be where we are today. And I am very fortunate to be able to relate our story to you.

My family and I will forever be indebted to the revolutionaries who fought and died battling against the brutality of a communist regime that enslaved our people. If it were not for their actions, my family and thousands of other families, would never have had the opportunity to seek freedom. My family will be indebted to those individuals who directly assisted us in our escape in Hungary, and those who helped us as refugees in Austria and Germany. It saddens me that my family and I no longer have record of who they were, or what happened to them. Finally, we will always be indebted to the people here in the United States, who, with their kindness, helped us in our assimilation into this culture. I will no longer be able to thank many of these people in person either. Most of them are gone. So in memory to them, I will be paying a debt of gratitude going forward.

My motivations for writing this family history have been to give credit and thanks to these individuals. I hope whoever reads this story understands the risks, sacrifices, and kindnesses made by so many people in order to help me and my family. I hope I've been successful in communicating my appreciation for them and their actions. So this writing is as much a thanks as it is a lesson to future generations to take care of their personal freedoms. Your liberty is the most precious thing you could ever lose. It is also the most wonderful thing you can ever win back. Like that pancake batter forming a perfect circle inside the confines of a pan, we immigrants are able to find ourselves and prosper within the liberties provided in the United States. That is something to cherish. God Bless America!

Béla (Bill) Suhayda
April, 2016
Sugar Grove, Illinois

Acknowledgments

A special thanks to the following people for their feedback and
support in the writing of this book.
A special thanks goes out to my mom Irén Suhayda who's memory
and attention to detail made it all possible.

Irén Suhayda
Lajos Suhayda
Brenda Suhayda
Stephanie Suhayda
Brett Suhayda
Joanna Suhayda
Les Suhayda
Joe Suhayda
Gyula Suhajda
Eszter Lovas
Olivér Sarkadi
Vito Carello
Ashley Bucchioni
Janet Henson Elliot
John O'Donnell
Matt Brennan
Beth Goins

CHAPTER ONE

The Escape

My grandparents' home
Godisa, Hungary
Nov. 20, 1956
4 A.M.

I t was an early morning. The sun hadn't broken over the horizon yet, and I hadn't slept well. I never did when my parents quarreled. This morning would become the most fateful morning of my young life, arguably, my entire life. My grandmother left with her son, my uncle Feri (Fare-ee) the night before. She was also upset that my parents were arguing. But I suspect it wasn't that my parents were arguing that upset her as much as what they were arguing about.

My father had made up his mind. He was taking his family and leaving this country. My mom fought his decision desperately. My father would remain undeterred. We were leaving this land, this culture, language, friends, and family. There wasn't going to be any changing his mind. The journey would start this morning. But where in the world we would end up was a mystery at this point even to him.

A revolution had raged in our capital of Budapest two short weeks before. The country remained in turmoil. The occupation forces of the Soviet Union had, miraculously, been driven from the capital and into the countryside by a civilian militia. The Hungarian people would enjoy freedom for seven short days. Then on November 4th, a Sunday, hundreds of Soviet tanks, accompanied by several brigades of infantry reinforcements, rolled back into Budapest to put down the revolt, killing thousands of men, women and children in the process. The hopes and dreams for the freedom of our nation crumbled into the rubble and smoke of our burning capital. An organized military waged war against a civilian militia made up mostly of college students, farmers, merchants, and ironworkers. It was David and Goliath all over again, only this time, Goliath would prevail.

Russian tanks roll into Budapest to put down the revolution

This revolution was as much about unshackling our nation from the repression of totalitarianism as it was about ridding the country of Soviet occupation. This revolt marked the first rebellion against communism in

Eastern Europe, giving collective socialism the black eye it so well deserved. It would eventually become the first action taken in Eastern Europe to rid the continent of communism. The Czechs (Slovaks) continued the process in '68. Lech Walesa in Poland would take the fight even further. Walesa, however, would choose a process of civil disobedience over bullets in his effort.

Freedom fighter

For communism, the writing was already on the wall, the Berlin Wall, that is, as it came tumbling down on Nov. 9th, 1989.[2] It was here in Hungary that the first domino toward that end fell thirty three-years and a day before, with the fall of this unsuccessful revolution.

"To the victor go the spoils" is an old adage often used to describe the gains made by the winners at the conclusion of a war. Hungary became a part of some of those "spoils" won by Stalin and Russia at the conclusion of World War II. The Red Army, with Franklin Delano Roosevelt's blessings, "rolled" into Hungary and the rest of Eastern Europe in 1945, and they never left. This revolt that had been put down just a week and a half

---

2 *This is the single most amazing historical event I can remember witnessing in my lifetime, and I'm almost sure that for me, it will remain that way. Up until it actually happened, I would never have dreamt that the end to the Soviet Union could ever have occurred, or the freeing of Eastern Europe from its evil clutches.*

ago, had been a fight for freedom from which occupation and a ruthless communist dictatorship was being "phoned in" by Nikita Khrushchev to a puppet government in Budapest. The Hungarian people desperately wanted their sovereignty back from their occupiers. So after a student demonstration in front of the Hungarian Parliament building ended with the AVO (Hungarian Secret Service Police) shooting into a peaceful and defenseless crowd of protesting college students, the only recourse left for the people was to take up whatever arms they could find against this savage communist dictatorship and defeat them.

Student demonstration just before the first shots were fired into the crowd

The situation in the country had reached critical mass. My father, along with the rest of the citizens of this unfortunate nation, had hoped for a much better conclusion to this rebellion. What hope the people had for freedom was now obliterated with the carnage of close to three thousand civilians in Budapest alone. A small window of opportunity for fleeing the country still existed but was closing quickly. This had been my mom's major objection to making our escape at this point in time. This had been the subject of the argument that sent my grandmother to my uncle's house. In my mom's mind, the time for leaving had passed. In her judgment, it was much too late and dangerous to do what my father proposed. We should have left immediately after the Soviets were driven into the countryside, my mom argued. The borders, which were open before, were again being guarded by the Russians. In my mom's estimation, attempting escape was much more perilous, if not impossible, now, than it had been just a couple of weeks before.

Many young people in the same predicament as my parents were still making clandestine plans for leaving this God forsaken country. The economic, social, and political conditions in the country were more than likely going to continue, with the failure of the rebellion. They could even worsen. For those who took an active part in the revolution, staying would be equivalent to suicide.[3]

It was in this frame of mind that my father decided that he had no future left in this country, and by that logic, neither did his family.[4] For many young people, the revolution created an opportunity for leaving. The country was in disarray. That chaos and confusion provided for a border less well guarded than before the revolt. In my father's mind, it was now or never for leaving. So without fanfare or preparation, my mom relented in this war of wills, and quickly packed three suitcases of our meager

3 *Fifty four years later, and after the communists had been driven from power, my cousin, Gyuszi Suhajda, took me through a graveyard in Budapest specifically constructed in the memory of the freedom fighters who had waged this revolution against the Soviet military. I walked through the expansive cemetery and saw grave markers of 18-year-olds who died in the years '57, '58, '59, and even '60. I asked my cousin why these people had died two, three and even four years after the revolt. His answer was disturbing to say the least. He indicated that these young people, who died years after the revolt, had only been incarcerated first. He explained further, that even 14-year-olds had been convicted and given death sentences for their crimes. Then, as these young people turned 18, they were executed by hanging or firing squad. Their bodies would then be delivered back to their families with a bill for the cost of their incarceration and execution.*

4 *My father managed the airport in Pécs (Pay-ch) after bouncing around from job to job following the end of the war. He wanted desperately to find a job in aviation. All of his training in the military had, of course, prepared him for such a career. He eventually succeeded in securing this managerial job in Pécs. But then for political reasons, he lost that job. He had been accused of using a government vehicle for personal use. It was a lie. The man bringing the charges had actually been the one who had done what he was accusing my father of doing. But this guy was in the communist party. It became an issue of my father's word against this communist bus driver's word. Party affiliation trumped the truth, and my father lost his job and his career.*

belongings and got us boys dressed. My father's 16-year-old niece, Etta, who was visiting with us during this time, said that she wanted to leave with us as well. We stepped out of my grandmother's house and into a cool dark November morning with our suitcases, never to return.

The early morning darkness gave us cover from the scrutiny of our neighbors. Leaving with luggage would have created unwanted questions in the light of day. It was common knowledge that people were escaping the country, but it was still illegal. Any person "abandoning" this communist state created a loss to this collectivist system. "Deserting" was equivalent to "stealing" from the people. In effect, anyone who defected, was willfully denying the country of their labor. Leaving was considered treasonous and punishable by a sniper's bullet through the head at the border. Individual rights did not exist under this form of socialism. A human life is only as important as their ability to contribute to the collective, under this system.

In these weeks after the revolution, many Hungarian citizens developed solidarity in ways that hadn't happened in recent history.[5] There was a rebirth of patriotism sweeping through the nation in defiance of the Soviets

5 *During the battles being waged in Budapest, we in the rural areas didn't know more than what government controlled radio stations told us. Of course they gave a very slanted version of the "truth." I remember my parents huddled around the radio listening to "Radio Free Europe" with the volume down so our neighbors would not hear. The only way the people of this country could know what was going on in their own country was through news reports from Radio Free Europe being broadcast from outside the country.*

and this communist government. One of the control strategies of this regime, over its people, was to encourage neighbor to inform on neighbor for speech or conduct against the state.[6] After all, there is little need for a government to strictly monitor its citizenry if everyone in the country is a potential spy. The paranoia created by this policy of pitting citizen against citizen, neighbor against neighbor, and even child against parent, had signs of breaking down in these weeks just after the revolt. Up to now, informing on your neighbor for talking against the regime, or other "acts of treason," were rewarded with good favor from those in power. The veracity of such allegations was of course unimportant. The major purpose of this government tactic was to create as much fear and distrust among the people as possible. The aim was to divide and conquer. Developing conspiracies for rebellion against the state is unlikely if even your child can turn you in for such disloyalty. Children were being taught, in these government controlled schools, to do just that. But things were changing. We would find our fellow citizens to be more than helpful during the three days of our escape.

A chorus of barking dogs, in backyards moved with us like a wave as we walked in the direction of the local train station. The sounds of the barking and our lonely footsteps are the things I remember most clearly. The early morning twilight covered the foothills of the Carpathian Mountains surrounding our village. The darkness concealed our clandestine plans as well.

---

6 *My cousin Gyuszi told me a story about a neighbor of his who had been reported to authorities for slaughtering his own pig. There had been a decree put forth by this communist regime that no one was allowed to slaughter any livestock for any reason without government permission. But this neighbor of Gyuszi did not want to risk a "No" from the local communist magistrate. He simply wanted to provide food for his family during the winter months. So he proceeded to sacrifice the pig for the cause. The pig, according to the new government mandate, was no longer his to slaughter. The pig belonged to the government as soon as the decree had been issued. Government agents came to the man's door, pulled him out of his house, and hung him from the nearest telephone pole. They left his body to hang within view of his family, and the rest of the public, for a week, so that all could understand the power of government mandates.*

My parents were not talking. The village was silent, still asleep. We walked past the one-room grade school that my older brother Joe and I attended. We were unaware that we would not attend another day of school there. Nor did we understand that we would never see our teacher, friends, or classmates again. We walked past my Uncle Feri's house where my grandmother went the night before. I wanted to say goodbye to her. Many years later I would learn that, just like me, she hadn't slept that night either. She had been awake and heard our footsteps as we walked past my uncle's house. She could not bring herself to come out to say goodbye. She had just lost her husband (my grandfather Menráth Mátyás) a month before. This morning she was losing her daughter and three of her grandchildren. She would return to her home later this morning to find us gone. Just two weeks before, there had been eight of us in her tiny seven hundred square foot home. Now the house was as empty as her soul. She was alone. She would not know, for months to come, where we were, if we had succeeded in our escape, if we had been arrested trying to flee across the border, or if we had been shot dead in that attempt?

Bagosi Néni (Mrs. Bagosi) and the classmates we left behind

It was a chilly November morning. The two-mile walk to the railroad station warmed us slightly. This station was the last one my grandfather managed before his retirement from the railroad. A locomotive, billowing steam and smoke pulling passenger cars, came hissing and chugging into the railroad station of our small village of Godisa (Go-dee-shaw). The rising sun created a silhouette of the massive engine and the gasses emanating from it. A dark acidic smoke that bit the inside of your nose poured from the smokestack. The engine shot white steam out of pressure valves on the sides and front of this dark metallic hulk. The shadow of the engine's smoke blocked the rising sun while the hissing steam loomed and condensed over our heads in the cool November air.

This is how I imagined fairy tale skies to appear when my grandfather read to me from his books about multi-headed fire breathing dragons. He recited many mythological stories to me about these horrific serpents and the brave Knights who fought them. My grandfather, in the last years of his life, suffered from dementia. The memory of his youth was still very much intact, however. Reconstructing what had just happened two minutes before was a much more daunting task for him. Nevertheless, he was amazingly entertaining, and a great story teller. While my grandmother cooked, washed, cleaned, fed the livestock, did the gardening along with a thousand other things including making all meals from "scratch," my grandfather read stories to me and told me about his youth. We lived in a world without television. My first glimpse of a T.V. would come in just a couple of months at Camp Kilmer, in New Jersey.

My grandfather read to me from colorfully illustrated books about beautiful young maidens kept captive by wicked kings and sorcerers. Handsome chivalrous young princes were always working to free young virgins from the evil clutches of hateful villains. It would take many thwarted tries, but eventually these heroes of yore succeeded in saving the young damsels from the dragons employed to keep guard over them. I remember sitting on my grandfather's lap, listening intently at his embellished voice, looking at the pictures and the printed pages I could not completely decipher. The plots of these stories were always about good conquering evil and the bravery it took to accomplish the dangerous rescues. I wanted to be just like these brave young men saving the beautiful princesses who were always gorgeous and always in peril. Little did I suspect that we would actually encounter and battle a multi-headed dragon in the form of this communist regime on this trip. Only decades later would I appreciate the perilous conditions we faced while fleeing this evil.

The train delays in the country became crippling for travel. Due to threats of sabotage of these tracks, the hold ups rendered the schedules to be meaningless. That would continue for the remainder of our journey. The tracks in this part of Hungary had been mined by the revolutionaries, or so went the story. Everyone suspected that it was this communist government that had put this "story" out. If anyone had mined these tracks, it was this regime. It made perfect sense. This tactic could only serve the regime. First, it discouraged people from traveling this specific route, which ran very close to both the Yugoslav and Austrian borders. It was across these two borders that most Hungarians were fleeing the country. Second, the blame for any inconveniences, injuries, or fatalities as a result of mine detonations would go to the resistance and their cause for freedom. The rebels had absolutely nothing to gain by mining these tracks. Delaying travel or getting citizens killed had nothing to do with what the revolution was about. To the contrary, the freedom fighters wanted to make it easier for people to defect. The rebellion was about freeing our people from occupation and communism. The fight was with this government, not the people. However, it was not out of the question to consider that this communist regime might stoop to placing explosives under these tracks and then blaming the rebels for the resulting death toll. Communists, Nazi's and other leftists had, and still have, long sordid reputations for such manipulated propaganda.

Train cars full of sand were being pushed onto "dangerous" sections of track. Train cars full of passengers would follow. Those rail workers unsympathetic to the government worked to keep the rails safe. Losing a rail car full of sand was preferable to getting people blown up. This first leg to Pécs (Pay-ch) had been slower than usual, and thankfully uneventful. We had two more days of travel before we would reach our crossing point close to the city of Sopron into Austria. We spent the remainder of this day in Pécs after only a short thirty-minute ride.

The Secret Service (AVO) agents at this stop began looking at my parents with suspicion. It was more than just a little unnerving given our "intentions." No questions were asked yet. But they were certainly scrutinizing our movements carefully. Then it dawned on my parents why they might be getting so much unwanted attention. They reasoned that it might have something to do with the black armbands they wore. In those days it was customary in Hungary for families to wear black armbands after the death of a loved one, and we had just buried my grandfather. Given the thousands of people who had been killed during the revolution, perhaps these SS agents were thinking that our family had lost a family member in the rebellion. If that was the case, perhaps we were sympathizers in the cause and a danger to them. It was not wise for us to draw attention to ourselves in this way and certainly not at this point in time. My parents discarded their arm bands post haste.

We boarded the next train for Barcs, (Barch) at around 6 in the evening after a 10 hour layover. The train limped along slowly and stopped in places where there was nothing but wilderness. Looking out of the windows and into the night, we could only make out the dark shapes of the mountains along with nondescript plains close to the Yugoslav border. The snail's pace of the train was annoying and nerve racking for those on board including my parents. My brothers and I were blissfully unaware of the situation as we slept through most of this slow creep into the late night and then early A.M. hour into Barcs.

Barcs, Train station
November 21, 1956
1 A.M.

We arrived in Barcs after midnight. My parents spent the remainder of the early morning hours before sunrise trying to get some sleep on the hard wooden benches in the waiting room. But their three boys were more energetic, having slept four or so hours since our departure from Pécs. We were being loud, running around, and a general nuisance to our parents and other travelers trying to get some rest. The next train traveling to Szombathely (Soam-but-hell-y) would be departing at 8 in the morning and we would be on it.

The train filled with passengers before the 8 a.m. departure from Barcs. Many among this group of travelers were middle aged and even elderly women carrying produce that would be sold at a farmer's market taking place in Szombathely the next day. We would pick up many more passengers like these at each stop before that destination. Among our passengers was also a large contingent of younger people-especially young men. Somewhat mysteriously, these men would leave the train at unscheduled stops and we wouldn't see them again. The warnings of the mined tracks had worked to slow the train in some places and even caused it to stop in others. That made leaving it easy and simple. Had the train moved at normal speeds, leaving it would have been much more difficult and dangerous. So the warnings of sabotage had indeed worked to discourage some people from traveling to escape the country via this route, but it definitely helped those who were much more bold to leave it. This happened especially qui kly when conductors came through our car to announce the conditions on the Yugoslav border to be favorable for crossing. The railroad workers were most definitely being helpful to those planning to defect. My father took note and would later employ this strategy of getting vital information, concerning the border, from a railroad employee when it came time for us to make our run. These rail workers were taking a tremendous amount of personal risk giving out this information. If anyone reported them for what they were doing, they would most assuredly end up imprisoned or worse.

These tracks were within four or five miles of the Yugoslav border, but our parents had no intentions of going there. Yugoslavia, like Hungary, was a communist country run by another dictator by the name of Tito. That was just one reason why my father was not taking us across this border.[7] He was also concerned that Tito would work to transport refugees going into Yugoslavia back to Hungary. We would later learn from Hungarians in the U.S., who escaped via this route, that Tito hadn't cooperated with the return of Hungarians who defected to Yugoslavia. My father was not assured, at this time, that that was the case. The other reason we were not going to Yugoslavia had to do with the distance we would have had to travel on foot to get there. Our parents considered the distance and conditions for the walk to be too lengthy and difficult for us kids. The terrain was treacherous even for adults. A part of that long walk would have needed to be in the dark of night.

We were headed for an area just south of Sopron (Show-prone) further north of here. The distance to the Austrian border was just a few miles from

---

7 *Yugoslavia was not a friendly place for Germans or Hungarians during World War II. My mother's brother had been made to "disappear" in 1944 for reasons probably relating to the fact he was German and that he was also a successful business man. It was the job of communists here in Yugoslavia, as was the case in Stalin's Russia to cull the population of capitalists and other undesirables in order to bring in their new world order. Tito's Partisans made lists of those not sympathetic to the communist cause which they were then allowed to eliminate. Menráth János, my uncle, was on one of these lists and was dragged from his home, never to be heard from again. Mass graves of the victims of these disappearances are being unearthed in different parts of Yugoslavia today. DNA taken from family members are being matched with the remains being found. My uncle's remains have not been located to this date. Molnár Tünde, an unborn niece of my uncles at the time of his disappearance, has written a book entitled "Elhurcolások" (Disappearances) in which she describes the events of her father, grandfather, and my uncle's murders at the hands of Tito's communist Partisáns.*

these tracks, and the walk would be much easier. Austria had also, just a year before, regained its freedom from Soviet occupation. It was no longer a communist country. But there would be a bit of irony crossing at Sopron. I would have no knowledge of this until many years later, but my father's oldest brother, Joszef, died as a prisoner of war in a Russian labor camp, just after World War II, in that area. We were seeking our freedom in the very place that my uncle had lost his life.[8]

Getting sleep on this trip, to this point, had become a luxury. With the exception of the four or five hours we boys had gotten before Barcs, we were somewhat sleep deprived. We had only taken cat-naps in the waiting rooms or on the trains. I hadn't slept the night before we left, and neither had my parents. My mom made friends with an elderly lady who boarded in Barcs, and being desperate for some good rest, my mom asked the old woman if we could bed down for the night at her home in Szombathely. The lady told my mom she would be glad to accommodate us, but she lived far from the station and it would be difficult for us to walk, with all of our luggage, to her home. She suggested a better solution. She had a brother and a sister-in-law who lived close to the station. She said she would accompany us

---

8 *My uncle Suhajda Joszef, having been in the military during the war, became a POW in his own country when the Russian army came in to occupy Hungary in '45. He was being kept prisoner in the northwest corner of the country close to Sopron. He was unable to leave the country to surrender to the American forces in Germany as my mother and father had. My uncle was in a work camp in which he was put to hard labor with very little nourishment. The family was very concerned about him so Pista (Peashta), another brother of my dad, went to see if he could get his brother freed. It was well known that the Russian guards could be bribed so Pista accumulated as much money as he could put together and went to see if he could get his brothers release. The bribery worked. Joszef was going to be freed. Then he refused to leave. Pista was dumbfounded and asked Joszef why he wasn't leaving with him. Joszef responded that there was a head count made of all inmates at the end of each day. For each inmate that was missing, there would be one prisoner executed. Joseph could not take that onto his conscience. Months later he learned he may be taken to another labor camp somewhere in the Soviet Union. It was well known that very few people ever made it back from such gulags. It was common knowledge that only the healthiest prisoners would be taken. He didn't want to be seen as healthy. So he purposefully brewed a tea concoction made of tobacco and drank it. It killed him.*

to their house and ask to see if we could stay the night with her brother's family.

We arrived in Szombathely at 8 in the evening, having traveled all day. The locals arriving home and those going to the market and visiting left the train. We were getting off as well, hoping to stay with this nice lady's sister-in-law and brother for the night. But before we could leave the train, the "helpful" conductor, who had given out border information just hours before, came into our car and announced that everyone had to leave the train at this stop. He sounded much more stern and official now as he barked out the orders he had been given to pass along to us. He informed us that everyone on board, including those traveling through, would have to leave the train and submit to a security check. We were told to have identification papers at the ready.

The young men who remained on the train, those who had not yet left for the Yugoslav border at the "unscheduled stops," started to take the sacks of produce from the women who came to the market and slung them over their shoulders. The women, understandably, started to become somewhat concerned for their property and the unsolicited help that was being heaped on them. But after brief whispered conversations, the ladies seemed to resign themselves to the inordinate amount of help they were receiving. Some of the bolder men even convinced the ladies to follow them as they hurried to the front of the "interrogation" lines that were forming and talked the AVO agents into allowing them quick passage. It was obvious to my parents, and to others who had traveled with us on the train, exactly what these young people were doing. They were engaging in a bit of subterfuge of course. By taking the burdensome sacks of fruits and vegetables, and putting them across their shoulders, they were impersonating people who would be going to market the next day. These young people had stealthily evaded the scrutiny that the rest of us now had to endure.

Security here was intense and AVO were everywhere, unlike Barcs. The weapons they carried hung heavy from their shoulders on thick brown leather straps. Emblazoned on their hats and olive green uniforms were the communist insignias made up of the red star and the hammer and sickle. As we exited our car, an AVO officer with a "gestapo voice" again instructed us to have our I.D.'s in our hands ready to present on demand.

Freedom fighters

The large collection of travelers from our train stood in amazing silence and long lines with heads slightly bowed as if at a funeral. My parents already guessed that the questions to be answered here would deal with the purpose of our travel and our final destination. They already fabricated our cover story on the train at the same time that the "produce exchange" was occurring. We stood at the back of the long and silent line. The answers my parents and cousin would be giving interrogators, had to be in agreement. Any group of people traveling together, giving contradictory answers to the same questions would not be going any further.

My mom took my hand to guide me along as she held my brother Les in her arms. I could feel the sweat on her palms. Her hand was freezing. I looked up at her face. Her gaze was straight forward with cold stoicism.[9] Seeing these secret service officers, with their weapons across their shoulders, added to her concerned look. But then everyone in these lines had that same look. Even people not plotting escape dreaded this procedure. They had that fearful look you get at having done something wrong, even though you don't quite understand what it might be. It is the way people with guilty consciences suffer, like when you look up to see a cop car with its lights flashing in your rearview mirror.

Perhaps these SS agents would purposefully find some irregularity with our papers, or some other technicality would be discovered or manufactured to be used as an excuse to question us separately. Tyrannical governments don't need a reason to arrest anyone. They simply find reasons to be abusive. Looking suspicious during questioning would be as good a reason as any for a person to be "detained." There were no civil rights here. There were no Miranda rights, rights to an attorney, or the right to remain silent. Habeas Corpus didn't exist here. Detention could and would be deemed necessary at the whim of any of these interrogators. Torture for information was common practice in this country. The torture of a prisoner's family members would definitely be on the table if the prisoner was not forthcoming with 'good and credible' information. Torturing the child of a prisoner, to seek their 'cooperation,' would not be out of bounds in the least.

We inched up in line getting closer to the area in which the AVO agents were doing their questioning. Then my mom realized she had forgotten the name of the town she was to give as our final destination. She went over all of the bluff answers she rehearsed with my father and cousin back on the train. She had all the other answers. But she was blank on this most important one. Her insides quivered. Nerves rendered her memory useless. The name of the village, she was trying to recall, was a neighboring town to our next stop. Ironically, it wasn't a place that was

---

9 *My mom was and continues to be a courageous woman. She stood up to Nazi SS officers during world war II when she tried to help some Italian Jews being transported through her father's train station. (I allude to one of these incidents in my mother's bio.)*

unfamiliar to her. My grandfather had been employed at a train station near this community. She had visited this town before. The harder she tried to remember, the more confused her thoughts became. We were too close to the AVO officers asking the questions for my mom to talk to my father about the name. Not wanting to risk being overheard or looking suspicious, she decided not to ask my father for the information she so desperately needed. She wiped her sweaty palms on the sides of her coat as she entered the roped off area with the interrogators at their tables. Her heart pounded hard in her chest. Her mouth was dry. When it was her turn to answer the AVO officers, she slowly stepped up to the table, breathed a deep breath, and tried to look as composed as possible. She presented her documentation and then, when she got the dreaded question, she gave the S.S. interrogator the name of the town where my grandfather had been manager, Kenyeri (Ken-yer-ee). She already made up a cover story for the discrepancy she had just been forced into in case she was asked about it further. If the AVO interrogators noticed her answers were not the same as my father's, there would certainly be many more questions. So in case she was interrogated further, she would simply explain that her plans with us children were different. She would say that she was going on without my father and cousin to visit an old friend in the town in which her father had been station manager. This of course would not work if we were questioned separately. Fortunately, the Secret Service interrogators hadn't made the connection between all the members of our family, or so we assumed, after reflecting back on this critical moment.

My father was in line before us and was the first to be questioned. Then came my cousin, and then my mom, with my brothers and I at her side. My Mom was the last to be questioned. We would never know for sure, but later we thought that perhaps the interrogators had linked my father and my cousin together as belonging to one group. Then my mom and us boys, perhaps, were considered a separate group. Etta and my father had given the same answers to the questions. So when my mom's answers didn't coincide with theirs, maybe she was assumed to be traveling with just her children.

Our last names should have told them we were all together. Had the interrogators not kept track of our last names? Had they not kept record of who, and how many were in our group? Perhaps the chaotic nature of the process, including the young men hurrying through the lines created confusion for the interrogators. Whatever the reason, fate worked in our favor. We dodged the proverbial bullet.

Casualty of the fighting

This heightened level of security made my father start to question everything we were doing. He became worried about the next stop and others down the line. So he suggested to my mom that she take us back home to Godisa on the next train. He would go on alone and check out the situation on the Austrian border. If he found things to be favorable, he would come back for us and we would make a second try. But if things looked to be too risky, he wouldn't "roll these dice" again. In that case, we would live out the rest of our natural lives very much as prisoners of this regime. But by now my mom regained her composure. Perhaps she was more hopeful now having successfully gotten out of the tight spot she just navigated. Whatever the case, she had, by this time, committed herself to this "mission." She told my dad: "We have come this far, we are not going to backtrack now to just do it all over again." My father recognized her resolve and agreed.

My mom's old lady friend was also taking a calculated risk to herself and her family in assisting us as she was. The evening's discussion with this kind family dealt mostly with what we had already gone through and what we were about to do. We got a full night's sleep and woke to a traditional Hungarian breakfast of peppers, kolbasz, (Hungarian sausage) and fresh out of the oven homemade bread. We gave our thanks and said our goodbyes. We wished everyone well and walked the short distance to the station. Amazingly, there were no security checks at the station this morning. We boarded the train at around 8 a.m. headed for an area somewhere short of Sopron.

Destroyed Russian tank

Szombathely train station
November 22, 1956
8 A.M.

J
ohn Fitzgerald Kennedy, the eventual 35th president of the United States, has exactly seven years and twelve hours left to live. We are getting on this last train of our journey. This final leg of our clandestine trip would bring us as close as we could hope to get to Austria. Sopron, if we chose to go that far, was a border town of size and importance. It would most likely have the kind of security we experienced back in Szombathely. So going all the way to Sopron was not something we wanted to do. We needed to leave this train before Sopron. We would then make our run, some time in the dark of night, in the open fields or brush between some insignificantly small village train station along this route and Austria. There were two very important bits of information we would need to garner before our attempt. Where were the shortest routes to the border? And where was it safest to cross? The safety issue, by far, outweighed any other concerns.

There had been many people arrested or shot to death trying to defect, before, during and now two weeks after the end of the revolution. The chaos, mostly in our nation's capital, took Soviet military security away from the borders and sent them into areas of the country where there was still a potential for revolt. Border security, for the time being, became less important for the Soviets than the internal stability of the country. This played in our favor. Tall towers had been erected on the borders from which the Soviet guards and snipers sat looking over the terrain. They had a bird's eye view of whatever or whoever was approaching. Prospective escapees, trying to flee, could be seen for miles in their approach.

Most people chose to attempt their escape by night. To foil this strategy, the Russian guards shot, what were referred to as "Stalin flares," into the night sky when they sensed there might be someone in the area at or near the border. The flares illuminated the terrain turning night sky into bright daylight instantaneously. If the Russian guards or snipers spotted you, they would command that you stop and surrender. But if you didn't surrender or if they didn't feel they could catch you before you could make your escape, they had orders to shoot to kill. The lazy ones who didn't want to climb out of their lofty perch to make arrests, or who didn't want to do the paperwork after an arrest, would simply shoot to kill.

Taking a page out of the book of the young men defecting to Yugoslavia, my father talked to the conductor on our train, asking him about the border situation along this area next to the Austrian border. Having witnessed the cooperation of train employees on our train the day before, he hoped that the goodwill he had seen from railroad employees the day before, might continue. If this man was a loyalist to the communist party, our journey would certainly end here and now.

The conductor told my dad he would get off the train at the stops and ask the managers of the depots, about the conditions that existed on the border. Naturally, he didn't want to be seen or heard by other passengers on the train as a person assisting anyone in this way. He indicated he would not be talking to us. He would stand outside the train car and give us a signal, through the window, about the situations that existed. He told my dad we should watch him for an "all clear" sign if conditions were favorable.

If things were good he would nod his head "yes." If conditions were not favorable, he would shake his head "no." We were to be ready to get off the train at any and every stop. We gathered our belongings together for a quick exit or perhaps a quick arrest.

There had been many shakes of the head for "no." But we hadn't been arrested yet either, so we understood we could consider our conductor to be trustworthy. Sopron was looming bigger in the window with every station. This train would not be going past Sopron. Sopron was the terminating station of this run. From there, it would make the return trip to Szombathely and eventually back to Pécs. We stopped eight, nine, ten times. None of the stops had been good locations for escape, for reasons we weren't made aware. We had one more stop before the end of this run. We knew that Sopron would be full of Secret Service and the end of the line for us. The only thing that would be left for us to do, at that point, would be to return home.

We arrived at a small village before Sopron called Sopron Pereszteg, (Pear-es-teg) our eleventh stop since we boarded the train this morning, before we got our nod to freedom. This had been our last chance before Sopron. "Lady luck" was on our side! My mom would later suggest that my grandfather's spirit had been with us on this fateful journey. "He was our guardian angel," she would tell us years later. Considering all of the things that could have gone wrong to this point, I had to agree.

The conductor held up the train for a short time as we got off. Even though we had been ready for a quick getaway, it still took us more time than for most to get off the train. Getting luggage, three small children, and three adults through the small door of the train car took a little bit of effort. It was no longer a secret, in the car, what we were doing. People guessed our intentions even though we tried to appear to be common everyday travelers. Perhaps these people had seen this scenario play out before along this route. This may have been a very familiar scene to these passengers in recent weeks. They showed their concern for us and the dangerous thing we were about to attempt. They gave us their blessings as we hurried down the aisle. The conductor stood looking at us on the bottom step of the train car as it started to move towards Sopron. He gave us a wave as we waved our appreciation back to him.

We stood alone on the platform as the train slowly pulled out of the station. People, looking back at us through the windows also waved. Their faces looked more troubled than hopeful. A few passengers had gotten off with us. They had already walked to relatives or friends for joyful greetings and speedy getaways into Pereszteg. We stood with our luggage at our sides, looking somewhat forlorn with no one to greet us, and no one to give us a ride. My father started walking over to the railroad manager who had given the conductor the "thumbs up" to get us off the train. He cranked up the gate of the railroad crossing by hand. On the other side of the station was an old man in a wagon, with a cow harnessed in. The old man sat atop his wagon full of hay, and looked our way.

"Do you need a ride?" the old man called out.

My mom, a little apprehensive about the question from a perfect stranger, didn't respond at first. The old man asked again. This time my mom found the courage to answer.

"Yes we do."

My father, having heard the old man's offer, asked the manager if the old man could be trusted. The manager gave us his second "yes" for the day. We gathered around the cart as the old man encouraged us boys to get on top. Our luggage was piled onto the wagon as well. The old man explained that the adults, including my cousin, would have to walk since the cow was not strong enough for a load bigger than what was on the wagon already. Then, as the cow pulled us away from the station, my mom noticed we were also moving away from the village. "The old man is taking us in the wrong direction," she thought. We were headed into a corn field behind the station and in front of what looked to be a forest at the top of a large hill in the distance.

"Aren't we going to the village?" my mom asked.

The old man pulled back on the reins to stop the cart.

"You want to go to the village?" he asked, a little perplexed.

"Yes."

"Don't you want to go to the border?" asked the old man.

Astonished and guarded that the old man understood what we were up to, she responded.

"Yes, but not until after dark," she said.

"The best time for you to go is during the day...right now!! The Russians guard the border at night. The Hungarian soldiers, who may be sympathetic to you, guard by day. Your best opportunity to leave is right now."

Guard tower on the Austrian border

The old man had laid out the situation before us in very plain terms. My parents looked at each other with confusion. They had not been ready to make this commitment so soon. They thought we would have more time to ready ourselves before nightfall. The reality of the decision had come too quickly. But this was very valuable information that the old man just gave us. It became obvious to my parents that now was not the time for thinking. It was time for doing. It was go time. So within moments of getting off the train, we were headed for Austria.

The cart was on the move again. My parents and cousin followed on foot. The recently harvested hay smelled fresh and sweet. I always loved hay rides. No road was too bumpy when you rode on top of a hay stack like this. The hard ground and the lack of good suspension on the cart was more than made up for by the soft swaying stack of hay that cushioned our movement across a very uneven terrain. We moved slowly up a hill on a dirt road away from the station and into a cornfield that had only been partially harvested. It was a sunny and clear day with a bright blue sky. The sun shined almost straight overhead, the temperature very mild for November. The sunlight warmed us. The smells and sights of this area reminded me of being back in our village of Godisa. I had no sense of anything dangerous.

Russian Border guards putting up barbed wire in order to slow the progress of Hungarians escaping the country

Then the wagon gave a jerk as the old man pulled off the dirt road he was following. He took a sharp turn behind a small hill and whispered for us to be silent. Within just a few seconds of what was obviously quick evasive action on the old man's part, we heard a jeep go by, carrying Russian soldiers. The sound of the jeep faded into the distance. It was the changing of the night guard. We heard them, but we never saw them. Much more importantly, they hadn't seen us. The old man had heard the jeep before we did and instantly understood the action he needed to take. We stood completely silent for a few minutes, our hearts pounding. We had come within the width of a corn tassel of being discovered. Dressed the way we were, and carrying suitcases in a location like this, would have been a DEAD giveaway of our intentions. When the sound of the jeep completely faded, the old man pulled back onto the dirt road and continued to move further up the long hill and closer to the forest. We would think back on this moment in years to come and understand that had the cornfield been fully harvested, we would not have had enough cover behind the small hill to completely conceal our presence. Perhaps it had been weather conditions that prevented the harvest. Maybe the farmer who owned the corn field was a procrastinator, or simply lazy. Whatever the reason, the unharvested corn became our salvation.

The terrain here was rolling and uneven, so it was not only a surprise to us when we saw two soldiers pop up over a hill, but also frightening, especially after what we had just experienced with the Jeep full of Russian soldiers. We couldn't tell if these soldiers were Hungarian or Russian from this distance. We had dodged one bullet a few minutes ago. What were the odds we would evade another? My parents were concerned, especially my mom. The old man remained cool. He seemed to know something we didn't. He slowly made his way off the wagon and went to meet the two border guards. Sitting in his more lofty perch on top of the wagon, he had seen the soldiers before my parents did. These were Hungarian border guards. This was the day patrol the old man told us about. The old man went to meet the soldiers in a proactive gesture. He told the soldiers our situation and then started to bring them back to the wagon.

"Well I guess this is the end," my mom suggested in a philosophical tone.

"Nothing is over yet," my dad responded.

It appeared to me that the old farmer had done this kind of thing before judging by how he navigated past the Jeep. Now the way he engaged these soldiers, it just seemed to be another day at the office for the old guy. And he had pegged us as defectors from the moment he set eyes on us.

My father struck up a conversation with the two guards. The conversation remained cordial and friendly. My dad served as a fighter pilot in the Hungarian Air Force during World War II. So perhaps the loyalty of one Hungarian soldier for another would work in our favor. My mom seemed relieved. She even had a smile on her face. Taking out his wallet and the change he had in his pockets, my father gave the soldiers two thirds of the money he had.

"I won't need this where I'm going," he told the soldiers. "It will be worthless there."

He had in his wallet all of the money he possessed in the world. All of the rest of our worldly possessions were in the suitcases. Our fate resided in the hands of these two soldiers. If they did their duty, as their military oath bound them to do, we would be arrested, and our string of good luck would come to an end. But once again, countryman would help countryman. Hungarians were not going to turn against their kind anymore.

My dad gave away most of his money to the two soldiers. Still these men could have taken our money and turned us in. If they were found out for letting us go, as it seemed that they were, they would end up in a court martial and perhaps even executed. The two soldiers now gave us a heading and directions on how to proceed towards Austria. The old man flipped the reins against the cow's back and for the third time, the cart moved up the dirt road towards the forested area at the back of the corn field. My dad smiled, and I think my mom felt relieved, at least for the moment.

We continued up the dirt path that the jeep full of Russian soldiers followed. Then after another few hundred yards or so, the wagon again came to a halt. The old man told us that he could not go any further. It was no longer safe for him to continue. He said that if he were spotted any closer to the border than we were, things could get very bad for him as well. He was, after all, aiding in our defection. Many people had been shot for much less in this God forsaken country. We all thanked the elderly gentleman for his help and kindness. He wished us well. We did the same for him. I thought my father had given the soldiers all of his money. To my surprise, he reached into his wallet, and gave the old guy the rest of his worldly fortune.

We didn't know it at the time, but we were less than a mile from Austria. The corn rows had dwindled down to just a few and we were now going to enter a section of brush on foot. The bushes and small trees gave us cover in case the guard towers were manned by Russian snipers. To the casual observer, this area may have seemed to be a quiet tranquil place, not a killing field where escapees had been murdered. The landscape was pristine with the exception of this field of corn. Most of the leaves were off the bushes and trees. It was very much a fall nature walk, something I might have done at home in a section of woods called the Libinca.

My parents were honest and transparent about what we were doing. We understood as well as any young children could about what we were up against. Now my dad gave us instructions on how to proceed. We were to stay close together. We were not to talk for any reason, and we were not stopping for anything. Now I had not gone to the bathroom since getting out of bed early this morning. And I was sensing an urgency to relieve a pressure that had been building for a while. I didn't say anything. Looking at my dad's serious face, I sensed that this was not the time or place to bring up my bladder situation. I understood very clearly that the longer we stayed in this area, the more precarious our situation would become. I held my tongue and my urine.

My older brother Joe went ahead of us with my father as he led the way into the brush. My cousin Etta took my hand and we followed behind. My mom had my younger brother Les in her arms as they followed my cousin and me. We lowered our heads as far as we could to stay below the tops of the bushes and small trees. We were in a fast walk. We had to move quickly to keep up with my dad, who moved faster than we could. Occasionally he slowed his pace and turned to urge the rest of us to stay close.

I remember back as a child, that I often did more than just listen to what adults, including my parents, would say to me. I also paid attention to how they said it. The tone of their voice, how they stood, and especially the look in their eyes, often said more than their words. I used to focus on the expressions on the face of my grade school teacher or my grandparents to get an idea of how much trouble I might be in. I found body language was always a better barometer of adult attitudes than words. As I looked at the expressions on the faces and movements of my parents and my cousin, it was very apparent to me, we were in danger. I smelled their fear.

The nerves I was experiencing were not in the least helpful to the urgency of my bladder situation. I knew better than to suggest that we stop so that I could hide behind some tree to relieve, by this time, an unstoppable force consuming every fiber of my being. We moved on and eventually the time came when I had no more control. I felt the "warmth" run down my legs and into my socks and shoes. I didn't utter a word remembering my dad's instructions to "keep quiet." And his other instruction, "We are not stopping for anything!!!" I felt humiliated peeing myself in front of my 16-year-old cousin. My embarrassment consumed me until I realized no one else took note of what just happened. If they had noticed or smelled my wet, urine stained pants, it became obvious to me they didn't care. It wasn't important to anyone but me. Suddenly my dad stopped dead in his tracks. We caught up to him as he looked at an old weathered wooden sign. At the top of the sign was the universal sign for danger, the skull and crossbones. Underneath was a message in Hungarian which read; "DO NOT PROCEED...AREA MINED!!!"

I remember my parents moving to the side and having a short, but very intense, whispered, conversation. My dad now turned to us and in a very quiet tone instructed us to follow in his footsteps as we moved through this area. We were to step nowhere else but where he stepped. The brush cover here prevented low lying grasses from growing up through the soil. As a result, the ground was bare in many places. Footprints in the clay soil were evidence that there had been others who recently made this dangerous trek before us. My dad followed in their steps.

Where were these people now? Had they been captured, shot, or had they made it through safely? Would we enjoy or suffer the same fate that they had? My father proceeded much more slowly now, and with obvious caution inspecting the ground for signs of any disruption of the turf. He looked for evidence of where mines may have been either picked up or laid down recently. He placed his feet where he saw other footsteps. When that wasn't possible, he looked for areas that were well established with vegetation. Time stood still for me. I have no recollection of how long it took for us to get through the area. I don't know if we ever became aware of where the minefield ended, or if it ever had. That information of course would not be posted. However long it was, this time seemed like an eternity for me. Then we heard faint voices in the distance. Our immediate thought was that we had been discovered. We crouched down and listened intently trying to determine from where these voices were coming. Then we heard women's voices and laughter. My mom listened carefully trying to make out the words. The voices were far away and faint. We could not make out the conversations. They didn't sound familiar. If these people spoke German, we had made it into Austria, or at least we were close. If the language was Hungarian, then we were still in Hungary. Was it possible we had gotten turned around somehow? Or had we ended up back in Hungary as a result of some irregularity of the border folding over itself? My parents' frustration grew, not being able to make out what was being said. Understanding the conversation or the language would be very helpful in determining our situation and where we were.

The first language my mom spoke as a child was German. After all, her parents were German. Even though they lived in Yugoslavia, they spoke German at home. The second language my mom spoke was Serbian, which she picked up before starting school. She was born in Yugoslavia and Serbia existed as a "region" or state belonging to Yugoslavia at the time. From a very tender age, she spoke two languages. Hungarian, by now, was her third language.

The voices became louder as we cautiously moved closer to their source. The fact that we were hearing women's voices gave my parents comfort. It was highly unlikely, even impossible, that border guards, especially at this time and place, would be female. Suddenly, my mom realized what language it was that she was hearing.

"It's Croatian," she whispered to my dad.

It was a dialect of the Serbian language she spoke in school in Yugoslavia. They looked at each other with confusion.

Staying low, we cautiously stepped out of the forest. We slowly walked into the bright sunlight and onto a section of plowed field, suitcases still in hand. Church bells rang in the distance. It was noon on Nov. 22, 1956. The tyrannical "Utopia" that had become a part of the communist experiment, in our home country disappeared behind us. Freedom reigned under our feet. Next to the narrow one-meter section of plowed field were small flags running to our right and left as far as we could see. The flags were all identical, and clearly defined the country we had just entered. They were red at the top, white in the middle, then red on the bottom.

"We are in Austria," my father announced.

Our relief quickly faded with my mother's yell.

"Oh my God, there is a dead man over here!"

She did not allow us kids to linger in the area.

"Take the kids away from here."

She directed my brothers and I away as she spoke the words. The unfortunate soul, lying face down in this field had made it to freedom, but lost his life as he stepped just a few yards onto Austrian soil. Had a Soviet border guard shot him while still on Hungarian soil? Had he managed to walk into Austria and then die of his wounds? Or perhaps he was shot dead right here on this spot by a Russian sniper from one of the guard towers. We would never find the answers to these questions. But if he had indeed been shot dead on Austrian soil, this murder was a war crime. Here was a poor unfortunate lying dead in this field. He had most likely attempted his escape the night before under the cover of darkness. In contrast, we stood under a noon sun, in broad daylight, alive and free. We had the old man, and his knowledge of the border situation, to thank for our lives and now our freedom.

Death and Revolution

The locals working the fields, who we had been hearing all this time, spotted us walking out of the brush a mere hundred or so yards away. They immediately started waving and yelling to us. At first it seemed that they were waving "hello," but my mom told us they wanted us to "Get down!" At the same time, other workers were beckoning with their hands, urging us to move toward them. It took us a while to understand what they were trying to tell us. They knew of the dead man just 20 yards from us. They wanted us to move away from the area as quickly as possible. They also wanted us to stay low. We lowered our heads and ran in a semi squat position until we got close to where these people were standing. They continued talking incessantly with their hands, feet, and loud voices. My mom translated as quickly as she could. They piled our luggage along with my brothers and I into a small cart being pulled by a tiny diesel tractor.

This was a Hungarian village before World War I. It was also a part of Croatia at one time. Now it was a part of a free Austria, which recently gained independence from the Soviets. The shell game of shifting borders as a result of all of the wars in Europe had brought people from at least three different countries into this village. The tyranny of communism made us the most recent arrivals to this multi ethnic community of Nikitsch.[10]

---

10 *One of the most dramatic shifts of borders in Europe took place at the end of World War I. With grave economic, political, and geographic consequences, Hungary lost two thirds of her territory and one half of her population in a "treaty" called Trianon. Nikitsch was known as Füles during the time that this village was a part of Hungary.*

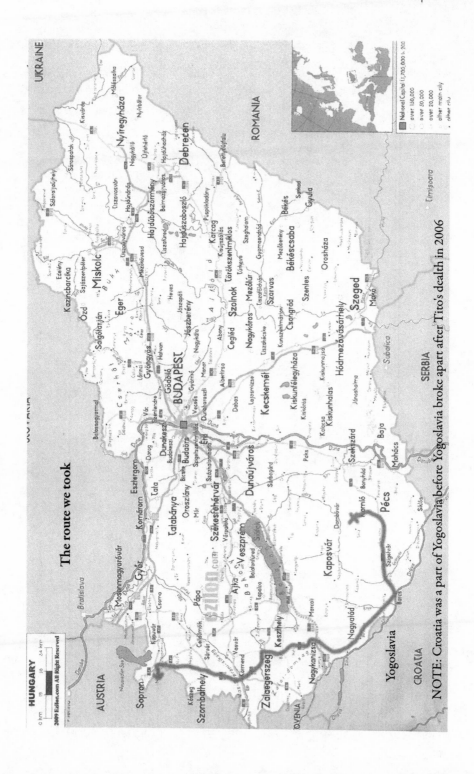

The route we took

NOTE: Croatia was a part of Yogoslavia before Yogoslavia broke apart after Tito's dealth in 2006

CHAPTER TWO

Living like a Refugee

Nikitsch, Austria
Nov, 22, 1956
12:05 P.M.

My brothers and I, along with our luggage, were loaded into a cart being pulled by a small diesel tractor. The bottom of the cart was covered in dirt. As the soil came in contact with my wet urine soaked pants, I turned into a muddy mess. Much to my relief, my parents were not concerned with my cleanliness at this point. The tractor spewed a sooty diesel exhaust, as it made its way into town. We arrived at a building where other refugees were already receiving food and shelter. I got a change of clothing. There were other Hungarian families who were already here in what we assumed was a makeshift refugee camp. These folks related their escape stories as we were treated to food and drink. A tall, slender, elderly gentleman who spoke impeccable Hungarian, went table to table waiting on the families. Full of exuberance and joy, he made his way around talking with everyone in the room. He smiled a big smile as he came to our table. He seemed to want to help us, and all of the others in any way he could. He was celebrating with us in our great fortune at making it to Austria, and freedom.

The man asked us kids what we wanted after our trip, and we didn't hesitate.

"Chocolate!" we told him.

My parents were astonished and embarrassed at our brash response, and told the old man to ignore our request. But he was insistent, and said that he would go to a local store and get us the candy we desired. I would later learn from my mom that this elderly gentleman had once been a man of wealth. He had probably left Hungary right after World War II, but had not made it any further west than Austria. With regime change and the advent of communism, Hungary had become a dangerous place for him. His major sins would have been that he was a man of wealth and privilege. People with money and position were routinely thrown into prison on trumped up charges in all communist countries in Eastern Europe after the war. Their homes and wealth, of course, were all "nationalized." All private wealth and private property under the previous government were confiscated. People of influence under the previous government and in previous governments were incarcerated or killed. This was done to make room for the "new world order" of perfect equity, and social justice under communism. It was a kind of political cleansing that despots like Lenin and Stalin made famous during their establishment of political power in Russia and Eastern Europe.

In Pécs, the city of my birth, there is a factory by the name of Zsolnay. The Zsolnay family built a world-renowned company for the production of porcelain and porcelain products. They produced some of the most beautiful china in the world dating back 200 years. I visited the factory in one of my more recent visits back to my native land. Oliver Sarkodi and his wife Eszter, who have become good friends of my wife Brenda and me, took us on a tour through a section of the restored factory that had been made into a kind of museum outlining the history of the company.

I read in horror how the owners of this family business had everything taken from them after World War II by the new communist regime that took over the country. Many of the family members were imprisoned and many died while in prison. Their business and personal property became state property overnight. It was the attitude of the communist despots and the proletariat of the time that successful people like these had stolen from the people. In other words," They hadn't built that." This is a sentiment that even our own very liberal progressive president (president Obama) has expressed when speaking of private businesses successes.

Many wealthy Hungarians saw the handwriting on the wall and left this now totalitarian state to go to Western European democracies where they could perhaps start over again. They left behind homes, businesses and anything else they could not carry. This elderly gentleman, having fled the country, escaped jail or murder at the hands of the communists. He now lived in exile here in Austria. It was this terrible, elitist, wealthy man who now delighted in getting us some chocolates at the local grocery.

From Nikitsch, we were loaded onto a bus headed for Eisenstadt. Eisenstadt was a processing stop for refugees. We were registered and given identification cards along with papers that authenticated us as temporary residents of Austria. Later that same evening, we were put on a bus and taken to a town near Vienna called Mödling. We arrived at a Catholic Monastery in the middle of the night. The monks and nuns came to retrieve us sleeping kids from the bus and took us to our rooms. We were one family to a room. There were four, maybe five Hungarian families being taken in by these monks in Mödling. The rest of the people on the bus were taken to other places in and around Vienna with similar accommodations.

This would be our home for the next three weeks as we waited for countries around the world to open their borders.

We had, of course, given away all of our money, not that Hungarian money would have had any value here. The monks had an old tractor destroyed by the Russian Army. The Russian army destroyed everything in their path in anger at leaving Austria. The tractor had been a casualty of their rage. My father, besides having been an aviator, was also a skilled mechanic. The tractor was a problem looking for a solution. My dad became that solution. He repaired the tractor for some "pocket money."

My dad put the tractor back into commission. The monks could not afford to pay much for the work. But they gave us free room and board, so my dad was willing to do the work even if they didn't pay anything. Nevertheless, they paid a small wage for the repairs. My mom took the money and purchased basic necessities along with some snacks between meals. One of the interesting foods she brought home with her were oranges. This was my first taste of citrus. I was amazed at how nature built an orange. I marveled at the little bite sized slices. My brothers and I enjoyed the sweet, juicy, acidic taste.

My mom's German came in handy in Austria. She became the interpreter for the refugee families here at the Monastery. My mom was at home even with the locals in town. Her German was so impeccable that many Austrians found it hard to believe that she was not German or even Austrian. The locals were all very kind and even curious about these strangers who had just come to town. It was very typical of them to give us chocolate candy as a way of welcoming us. It was our pleasure as gluttonous little refugees for eating up all of the chocolate and attention that was being heaped on us. All of this very rich dark chocolate finally became too much of a good thing for me. To this day, I avoid chocolate in any other form than maybe a brownie here or there. No more bonbons for me.

Then one day, in our second week in Mödling, I started running a fever. It got worse with time. I started sleeping a lot and going in and out of consciousness in a delirious state. Time became irrelevant. I didn't know day from night. About the only thing I remember of this time is my mom putting cold compresses on my forehead. Things must have gotten pretty bad because an ambulance was called for me and I was rushed to a Vienna hospital. For my parents to send for an ambulance, things must have been quite dire. When we got to the hospital, a short bald doctor in a wrinkled white lab coat performed my examination. I still remember the examining room being very cold and blindingly white. It smelled of alcohol and ethyl ether. I sat half naked and shivering violently on the examining table as the old doctor listened to my heart, looked into my eyes, ears, nose and finally down my throat. Then he started tapping on my knee. He kept hitting me with this wooden mallet. It was getting annoying and even a little painful. I don't recall complaining about his drum solo, however. But I do remember the serious look on the old doctor's face, as he looked at my mom during this part of the examination. He wasn't getting the responses from me that he thought he should be getting.[11]

Many years later (early seventies), in a Human Physiology class at Aurora College, Associate professor Ron Kimmel called me up to the front of the class. I was to be his "guinea pig" in a demonstration of the "Patellar Reflex." The topic of the week had to do with the Central nervous system. On this particular day we learned about the "reflex arc". On my way up to the front of the classroom, I warned the good professor that I was not very proficient at this sort of thing. He looked at me with a wry smile of amusement. I think he thought I was trying to be funny. To a certain degree that was my intention as I thought back on this examination in Vienna and the doctor smacking me repeatedly and getting no response. How can anyone possibly be "good" or "bad" at reflexes I thought as I slowly walked

---

11 *The purpose of checking for a patellar reflex is to determine the 'integrity' of the nervous system. When the patellar tendon is struck, it gets stretched slightly. Stretch receptors in the tendon send a message to the spinal cord. After a couple of synaptic junctures, a nerve impulse comes back from the spinal cord to the quadricep muscle causing it to contract moving the lower leg.*

to the front of the classroom? It isn't as if it is something we can practice. It's an involuntary response, and by definition, beyond our ability to control.

Professor Kimmel prepared a tall chair for me to sit on. He asked me to dangle my right leg loosely as I took the seat.

"This is going to hurt you more than it does me," the professor joked.

I noticed the technology for "reflex mallets" had improved since my refugee days of Austria in the fifties. This mallet, unlike the Austrian sledge hammer of my youth, was rubberized. Professor Kimmel struck me gently just below the kneecap on the patellar tendon and got...you guessed it... gar nichts... nothing...nada...zilch! Again, he asked me to relax my leg and the quadricep muscle specifically. He struck the tendon again, and still nothing! I asked him if he thought I might be dead?

Back in that sterile doctor's office in Vienna, my mom told me to relax my leg as the old doctor continued to play "knick knack, patty whack," on my knee. The doctor, now looking at my mom with concern, exchanges words with her in German. My mom looked back at the old doctor with alarm. I failed this last, vital test of the doctor. He was not getting a patellar reflex. He ordered me to be kept for observation at the hospital. I would be admitted this evening. I was not going home. My parents would be leaving without me.

When they visited the next day, they were not allowed in my room. They could only look at me through a small window in the thick metal door. I saw tears in my mother's eyes as she tried talking to me through the small window. Seeing her tears made me cry. I was getting very concerned about what was going on. I could barely make out what my mom tried to say through the small window in the door. I wondered how sick I might really be if they didn't allow my parents into the room. I was actually starting to feel a lot better with the medication the nurses were giving me. It seemed my fever had broken. I was no longer delirious. I couldn't understand why I was being kept in this hospital and away from my parents.

I felt much better. But I remained cut off from almost all human contact for some very strange reason.

The only things I had to keep me company throughout this very long week of hospitalization were a bunch of stuffed toys including a very cute button-eyed teddy bear. Because of my tender age, I had been placed into the pediatrics ward. I felt a little silly surrounded by stuffed animals and a bed that looked too much like a crib. After several days of almost total isolation from human contact, I actually started to form an emotional attachment with my furry little friends, especially the teddy bear.

I was most assuredly quarantined. Although I had no understanding, or such a word to describe my loneliness, I certainly understood how it felt. I was a leper. Nurses came into my room, covered head to toe swishing around in their starched white uniforms. On top of their bun covered heads were little white hats. Surgical masks covered their mouths and noses. I couldn't tell one nurse from another. They all looked as if they were about to commit some kind of crime. When they left, they locked the door behind them. The sound of the latch, as they turned the key, was not only isolating, it was scary. I felt imprisoned. I had no companionship except for my teddy bear and the brief visits from the nurses when they came in to check my vitals or bring my meals. I hadn't seen my parents for days. None of the nurses spoke Hungarian with the exception of a couple of words that I had taught them for hello and goodbye. They tried hard to communicate with me in German. I stared at them in confusion.

A few days before my discharge, the nurses are no longer wearing their surgical masks as they come into my room. I can see their faces and their great smiles. They no longer lock the door on me when they leave. Sometimes they even leave the door wide open. The nursing staff spends more time with me. I'm starting to pick up on some words and expressions in German. Gott im himmel! My parents are now allowed to come into my room and I can talk with them without a door between us. I plead with them to take me with whenever it comes time for them to leave. My mom promises that I will be going with them very soon. It will take just a couple of more days, before my discharge she says.

I received my discharge from my aseptic prison a few days later. My little teddy bear and his fuzzy little friends had become my firewall against loneliness. Deep in my gut, I sensed it would be very difficult for me to part with them once the time came for me to leave this place. Instinct told me that this was going to become a source of embarrassment for me. Cautiously I asked my mom if she could arrange for me to take my loyal little friends with me. But the hospital staff told my mom other children would need the cuddly little guys just as I had. At first they weren't going to let me take any of my little friends. Tears ran down my face as I begged not to be separated from my friends. My mom attempted to discourage my crying by suggesting that I was too old to have such an attachment for toys. But after my teary display, the nurses relented and allowed me to take my button eyed Teddy with me. The hospital staff were all smiles, wishing me well as my parents and I walked out through a kind of tunnel to a waiting vehicle going back to the Monastery. The hospital staff had been as attentive to me as they could, given the situation. I was grateful to them all for all of their attention, and especially for my little friend that they let me keep.

As it turned out, the old Austrian doctor had not done a very thorough examination of my condition. How he missed my infected tonsils, when he looked down my throat, my parents would never understand. Because of the lack of a patellar reflex and a very high fever, the old doctor diagnosed me with spinal meningitis. Getting a more thorough family history would have helped in his diagnosis since it turned out that my dad also had tonsillitis during this same time. He passed the infection to me somehow, probably the oranges. In a relatively short amount of time, I played street soccer with some of the Austrian kids in the Monastery neighborhood. I think one of them may have been Arnold Schwarzenegger.

Many years later, as an adult, watching the movie "Cast Away" brought back the feelings associated with this hospital experience very clearly. Tom Hanks' character is stranded on a deserted island somewhere in the Pacific after a plane crash. Slowly but surely, loneliness creeps into his life, as it had into mine. He paints a face on a volleyball that survived the crash with him. He gives the ball the very unimaginative name of Wilson, the name of the manufacturer of the ball. The humanoid face keeps him company as he makes conversation to it throughout his isolation on the island. One of the saddest moments in the movie is when Hanks' character loses Wilson on the high seas as he is leaving the island in search of a rescue ship. He watches Wilson float away from him into the open sea with no hope of ever being able to retrieve him. His heart breaks as he loses the only friend he has known for years. I understood his desolation perfectly.

Every morning...the nuns served us hot chocolate along with a slice of rye bread. This was breakfast for the pious. I spent a lot of time "religiously" picking the rye seeds out of the coal black bread. I hated the harsh "minty" taste of these horrible tasting little seeds. For me, biting into this bread, with the rye seeds, was akin to biting down on a piece of eggshell in your scrambled eggs. My childish concerns dealt with terrible tasting bread. My parents' adult concerns dealt with where in the world we were going to live the rest of our lives.

Almost 200,000 Hungarians left Communist Hungary during the revolution. 188,000 of these people escaped to Austria. Only 12,000 went to Yugoslavia. The fact that Yugoslavia was communist and Austria was a free country had a lot to do with why we and other refugees were here. The head priest at our Monastery spoke to the families who took up refuge here with this Catholic institution. He told the families, including my parents, that they needed to visit the embassies of the countries to which they wanted to emigrate. We were to go to Vienna and register with the embassies of the countries that would open their borders to us.

Richard Millhouse Nixon, Vice President of the United States at the time, came to Vienna to assess the refugee situation. The U.S. was going to accept a certain number of Hungarian immigrants. Many Hungarians, including my parents, were very uneasy establishing permanent residence in Austria or Germany. They felt fearful staying in a country so close to the Soviet Union. The Russians had only just left Austria after occupying the country since 1945. What assurances did refugees have that the Russians would not return? The sense of most refugees was that there needed to be a large buffer from the Soviets and the evils of communism. Austria and Germany were considered too close for comfort by many refugees to stay in this region of the world.

My parents registered with the embassies of Canada, Australia, and the United States. Now they waited to see which country opened their borders first. Their plan was to go to the first country that opened its borders, with a slight preference for the States.[12] Congress acted to open the U.S. to limited immigration. After three weeks in Mödling, we were on our way to America.

We were bussed to a train station very close to the Hungarian border. We were so close in fact, that on our way to the station, some refugees on board became concerned that they were being deported back to Hungary. People could see into Hungary from where they sat on the bus. We were assured by our driver that we were not being taken back. The reason for bussing us and the many hundreds of other refugees to this remote train station had to do with our huge numbers. The entire train's population was refugees. We were 1,400 strong. The logistics of putting such large numbers of people onto a train, in a major railway station in Vienna, would have

12 *My parents had been in a POW camp in Germany, right after the war. My mother accompanied my dad and his Hungarian flight squadron to Germany where they surrendered to American forces. Surrendering to the Russians would have been suicidal for my dad and very dangerous for my mom. Russians threw Hungarian soldiers into labor camps in which they were starved and worked to death. Also, Russian soldiers raped the women of the countries they invaded. My parents were very appreciative of how they were treated during this time in U.S. captivity. They saw American soldiers as very humane and decent people. My parents remembered this when it came time to choose where in the world they wanted to go.*

been a huge inconvenience to Austrians traveling to or from Vienna. So it was decided by Austrian authorities that we would use this more remote station.

This would be a long train ride, with a couple of stops on the way to a major shipping port in Germany. We were going to be boarding a ship in Bremerhaven headed for the U.S. When the train made its scheduled stops, the German people would come to our windows waving their hands and giving us little packages of food that they prepared for us. It seemed these people expected us. In Germany, as in Austria, we felt a support and a solidarity with those who helped us. There was a genuine concern by the people of Austria and Germany for what we had done and what we were going through. People of both countries understood the dark regime we escaped. Now they celebrated our freedom with their generosity, as we looked to find a home somewhere in the free world.

We reached the port of Bremerhaven. My parents told us we were going to be traveling on a large ship and crossing the Atlantic Ocean to America. But my limited imagination had not been large enough to accommodate the immensity of the Atlantic Ocean or the ship that would be transporting us across its very rough surface. The ship was so huge, I couldn't see its entirety in one glance. At first, I didn't even recognize it as a ship. Only after a second and then third glance in one direction, and then another, did I recognize it for what it was. How could anything this huge float, I wondered. Whenever I had gotten into water, I sank. Buoyancy was still a foreign concept for me.

Bremerhaven, Germany
December 24, 1956
Early morning

A long line of people grew, extending for hundreds of yards from the gangway of the U.S.S. General W.G. Haan. All 1,400 of us who were on the train, now boarded the ship. A black woman (this was the first black person I had seen) spoke to us in Hungarian saying; "God welcomes you to America." As the ship slowly floated away into the harbor, a band on shore played the Hungarian National Anthem. It was followed by the Star Spangled Banner. There wasn't a dry eye on the ship. All on board were moved by the music and this thoughtful gesture on the part of the U.S. government. Many on board had not yet processed the enormity of the decision we made in leaving our country. Our hectic and chaotic movements as refugees through Austria and now Germany hadn't given us much time for reflection. The weight of the decision to leave now fell on each man woman and child. Not only had we left our beloved country, we were also leaving this hemisphere. Our national anthem now evoked the emotion that had not had time to surface. Would we ever be back here again? Would we ever see our families and loved ones we left behind? Would I ever see my grandmother again? The enormity of the decision we made now caught up with all of us. I haven't seen so many people crying all at one time since.

*U.S.S. General W.G. Haan; Troop transportation ship
that we were transported to the U.S*

We moved out into the chill of the North Sea. The shore line shrank away and finally faded from sight altogether. I had never seen so much water in my short seven years of life. The North Sea extended as far as the eye could see in all directions. The General Haan rose out of the water like a skyscraper when I had first seen it in dock. Now it nestled into the waters of the North Sea like a bird into its nest. We were taking on ballast to lower our center of gravity against the huge waves of the North Atlantic. We readied ourselves to be tossed around like a cork at the end of some fisherman's line. When I looked over the side close to shore, we were so high up that I got a slight case of vertigo. Now, it was almost as if I could touch the frothy waves as they moved quickly from bow to stern. Coming up ahead was the English Channel. After the Channel came the open ocean of the Atlantic. But before we got there, we got a glimpse of the White Cliffs of Dover. I saw a movie of these same cliffs, years later as a senior at East Aurora High School. I would learn they were made of chalk. They were the remains of countless numbers of microscopic organisms called coccolithophores. In chemistry class, I would learn that the compressed shells of these organisms were made of Calcium Carbonate ($CaCO3$). The formation of these shells act as a "sink" for Carbon Dioxide entering our atmosphere.

The U.S.S. General Haan could never be confused with a luxury ocean liner. She had been a troop transport ship at the end of World War II. The living quarters for the captain and his ensigns during war time were in the middle of the ship and above the water line. They were private rooms that slept three to four officers. The living space for the soldiers, which this ship normally carried, were usually below the water line and in the bow and the midsection of the ship. It consisted of hundreds of hammocks on which these military personnel would sleep. It was a stifling place without windows. This ship was designed to transport soldiers, not families and small children. So men and women were segregated to different parts of the ship. There weren't enough rooms to house each individual family. Privacy came at a premium. Women and younger children, of course, got the "luxury" spaces. Chivalry was still alive in the 50s. My younger brother Les and I stayed with my mom. My dad and brother Joe went with the men and older boys. They were relegated to the hammocks in the bowels of the ship where neither the moon nor the sun ever shone.

We spent two very long weeks on the Atlantic. It seemed we were paddling "upstream" all the way. We encountered some highly energetic storms. We had rough nights in which we strapped ourselves into our beds. There were actually seat belt type devices designed to keep us from falling out of our perched bunk beds. My brother Les, at four years of age, slept in a crib in the middle of our room. The crib slid back and forth across the room until one night, it folded up like a cheap accordion. It was like an Easter egg hunt in the mornings as we searched for where our shoes slid during the night. Meal times could be especially challenging as our plates slid side to side on cafeteria styled tables. Plates of food, you hadn't ordered appeared in front of you, having traveled enormous distances across the table. But if you had the patience to wait just a short few moments longer, you might see your original plate slide back to you. Keeping your food down was a gastronomic challenge.[13] Climbing up stairs could become effortless if you timed your climb during a period when the ship was falling away from you. It was advantageous to wait out the time when it moved in the opposite direction in which you wanted to move when climbing or descending steps to change floors.

We arrived in New York on the evening of Jan. 7, after having spent New Year's Eve and New Year's Day in the middle of the Atlantic. For whatever reason, we were not allowed to dock until the next day. We sat in the harbor after we dropped anchor. Everyone wanted off of this aquatic roller coaster in the worst way. The next day, as we left the ship, people kissed the ground, vowing never to travel the open seas again.

We were back on a bus, traveling and gawking at this "new world" through the windows on our way to Camp Kilmer, New Jersey. Ellis Island was closed for renovation. These were our first looks and impressions of the magical world called America. The skyscrapers we saw first from the harbor and now from the bus convinced us of the magnificence of this country. Most of us came from small villages with rural routines and simple lives. Here, we were looking at buildings fifty and sixty stories high. Even in major European cities like Brussels, Vienna or Paris, buildings rarely extend past ten stories. We strained to be able to see the tops of the buildings from our narrow windows as we drove next to them on the bus. The cars, the shops, the buildings, and airplanes in the sky were ubiquitous. No one on this bus had ever seen anything like this before.

My grandmother always washed our clothes by hand, back home. She hung the clothes on a line to dry. She brought wood or coal in for the stove to cook. None of us had ever owned a phone. Here, we would learn about washers, dryers, gas stoves, central heat, AC, and telephones. Here, our water came from a faucet in the house instead of a well in the back yard. Here we had indoor plumbing. There would be no more going out into the dark of night or the cold of winter to use the toilet. We had television for

---

13 *Almost everyone on board got sea sick at one time or other. I got very close on one occasion only. For the most part, children do much better than adults in this regard.*

entertainment. This was a very different and amazing world indeed. This was America.

CHAPTER THREE

Becoming an American

Camp Kilmer New Jersey
January, 8, 1957
Middle afternoon

We were processed as legal residents of the United States at Camp Kilmer military base in New Jersey. The camp served to house Hungarian refugees until we could settle in a community somewhere in the country. Companies, municipalities, and community organizations in the U.S. worked with the government by notifying them of openings for skilled and unskilled labor around the country. Refugees signed up for whatever openings they thought they could qualify. We would then be put onto military style buses and shipped to the communities offering employment.

Vice President Nixon visited Camp Kilmer and even addressed us in a speech. He visited us in Vienna just a month before. He kept President Eisenhower and Congress informed of the conditions at the camp and the progress being made in our "resettlement." Many people were feeling the frustrations of the long waiting process, as were my parents. People wanted to get some purpose and permanence back into their lives. A monotonous routine was preferable to any more waiting or any more travel. We were on the road now for just over two months. There didn't seem to be any end to the temporary conditions in which we found ourselves.

My parents made friends with the Boczko family back at the Monastery in Mödling. We were on the same train with them to Bremerhaven and had also made the two week "ocean cruise" across the Atlantic together. Mr. Boczko now told my parents that they were scheduled to leave the camp for a place in the north central part of the country. The name of the community was Ishpeming, Michigan. He said there was a community organization there that sponsored them, and that they were leaving shortly. My parents were also anxious to leave the camp. Not wanting to be separated from friends in this new country, they told the Boczko family we were leaving with them. We got our things together and went with the Boczko family to the bus that would be taking them to the U.P. of Michigan. But when we were about to board the bus, we were told by the clerical worker assigned to the seating, that all of the seats had already been preassigned. Our names did not appear on his list. But he gave us a ray of hope when he suggested that if there was anyone who didn't show up to claim their seats, we could have them.

The bus was almost totally filled. The time for departure came and went. There was only one family that hadn't shown up. We stood, poised for opportunity. Then after a few more minutes of waiting, the soldier with the passenger roster told us we could board. The unclaimed space was ours.

Eisenhower would go down in history as the man who lead the allied forces to victory over Nazi Germany during World War II. He would, of course, also go down in U.S. history books as becoming the 34th president of the United States. A much lesser known, but very important accomplishment for the president, would be the establishment of an Interstate freeway system that would run coast to coast making commercial and private travel in the U.S. much quicker, safer, and easier. He signed the bill in June of 56. But of course construction on the huge infrastructure project was still only in the planning stages. Our trip from New Jersey to Michigan was not going to be on a sleek, fast freeway. It was going to be a long and arduous "milk run" of a road trip on a "no frill" military vehicle.

After the two day bus ride, we arrived in Escanaba, Michigan. The date was Jan 27, 1957. There were 47 of us who made the trip, 48 if you include the baby about to be born to a young pregnant woman making the journey. All of these people were being sponsored by the Rotary Club of Ishpeming, Michigan, except us,... at least not yet. We became stand-ins, "stowaways" if you will, as a result of the family that hadn't shown up to claim their seats back in New Jersey. The Rotary Club expected a baker to be among the 47 refugees coming to them. But the baker hadn't made the bus. Maybe he was making donuts when he should have been boarding a Greyhound. So instead of getting a cake maker, they got my dad who was a mechanic/welder/pilot/handyman and a "jack of all trades." The newspaper account in the "Mining Journal" blamed government bureaucracy for the mix up. In actuality, the error had more to do with my father's determination at getting on the bus than with a government employee allowing us to take the place of the baker and his family. It may have been a "six of one and half a dozen of the other" kind of situation, with a slight edge to my father's stubborn insistence to get out of the refugee camp ASAP. With my dad, there was always a will, so there was always a way.

The Rotary club was not going to send us back to New Jersey. They were stuck with us. It was my mom's language skills, here, as in Austria, that probably made us a little less dispensable than the other refugees with whom we made the trip. My mom realized there were problems with communication between the refugee families and the Rotary club members. So she started to help with translating Hungarian to German between the dignitaries of the Rotarians, the press, and the rest of the refugees. There was another young Hungarian man (Joe Mraz) who was the translator up to this point, but his German was limited, resulting in some miscommunication. My mom noticed the difficulties, so she involved herself in the discussions. Mr. Voegler, an Ishpeming Rotarian, translated German to English, while my mom translated Hungarian to German. My mom's language skills may have had a lot to do with our eventual celebrity status at this event. She was key to bridging the communication gap between this collection of refugees, Rotary members, and the "Mining Journal" newspaper. We, in fact, became the feature story of the event.

SOME OF THE 17 HUNGARIAN refugees who were resettled in the U.P. on Jan. 15, are pictured as they walked from a bus into Holy Name High School, Escanaba, after trip from Camp Kilmer, N.J. (Photo courtesy Escanaba Daily Press.)

Our arrival in Escanaba Michigan

We stayed at a hotel for the night in Escanaba, Michigan. The next day we were picked up by Rotary club members and made the 70-mile or so trip to Ishpeming, where we were greeted by more members of the Rotary and former Mayor Emil Aho and other dignitaries of the community at the Mather Inn.[14] We, along with the other Hungarian families who would

14 *The Mather Inn and Ishpeming would become the backdrop to a very famous Otto Preminger movie titled "Anatomy of a Murder" filmed in '59. It starred Jimmy Stewart, Ben Gazzara, and Lee Remick. Interestingly, the film was based on a true story written by John Voelker. Voelker was, in fact, the defense attorney in the courtroom drama depicted in*
(cont. on next page.)

reside in Ishpeming, were treated to a social hour with the press and a formal dinner. My brothers and I were sent to our hotel room, where our parents would join us for the night after a social hour in the main dining room of the Inn. There was way too much excitement for us to go to sleep, however. Hotel rooms for us were a novelty, as were phones. We would pick up the phone and listen to hear if anyone was talking. Of course, the switchboard operator would come on and speak with us.

Not understanding a word, we would get scared and hang up immediately. We knew, intuitively, that we were doing something wrong. We knew we should not be playing with the phone. But we couldn't help ourselves. It was much too interesting, amazing and fun to put the receiver to our ear and giggle in anticipation of the operator's voice. We did this a few times before my mom walked into the room and told us to stop playing with the phone. Now how did she know we were playing with the phone, we wondered. When we denied having played with it, she told us the operator had told her it was us. For a long time, it would stay a mystery to me how the operator could tell it was us in this room playing with the phone. I had no understanding of a technology that could identify what phone in the hotel was being picked up at any time. Indeed this was my first experience with a phone in my young life. My mom brought us some popcorn and told us to eat it and then go to bed. She left again to "hobnob" with the "important people". Tasting this mysterious stuff called popcorn was another first. We fought over every morsel. Of course my older brother Joe would win most of these battles well into junior high and even high school. This is how it would be in our first years in the U.S. Everything was a mystery, a novelty, or a discovery. And it was all amazing!

From time to time, I think back to these early days when my family and I were first discovering this country and culture. The late 50s and early 60s evoke special memories for me. They were pivotal times for us. It wasn't as much culture shock for me and my brothers as it was a time of

the movie. He was also a Rotary Club member and eventually became a Michigan Supreme Court Justice.

revelation. Elvis was the rage of every teenaged girl including my cousin Etta. The Beatniks represented a counterculture and were satirized as a lazy lot in a sitcom called "Dobie Gillis." Chuck Berry, Fats Domino, and Ray Charles were dominant forces in the music world of rock and roll and soul. The "Doo Wop" music genre of the 50s was all the rage. For my parent's generation Perry Como, Frank Sinatra, and Dean Martin were tremendously popular. Marilyn Monroe represented "sensual innocence," while James Dean was a rebel without a cause in the movie by the same name. We became a part of what was to be termed the generation of innocence. We tuned in to sitcoms on TV like "Leave it to Beaver," "Father Knows Best," and "Ozzie and Harriet". Jack Benny and Bob Hope did stand up comedy. The Lone Ranger and Roy Rogers showed us how to fight against the outlaws. Superman could leap tall buildings in a single bound. Mickey Mouse loved Minnie Mouse and all kids loved cap guns and BB guns. Baseball great Joe Dimaggio had retired and Mickey Mantle and Roger Maris were on the rise with the Yankees. I look through family photo albums of these days, and experience all over again how it felt to be in this wonderful country during those, our early formative years. The people of the Rotary club, who helped us and cared for us in the first year and a half of our assimilation were some of the most caring people we could have ever hoped to know. I still feel a debt of gratitude to them.

Rested after their long tiring journey from Camp Kilmer, N. J., the three sons of Mr. and Mrs. Mati Suhajda — Leslie, Joseph and "Bill" — appear bright-eyed and eager to start making friends in their new country, far from Communist-persecuted Hungary. — (Homburg photo)

Us boys in our hotel room

We came from a world without running water in our homes, to a country where everyone drove in a car. No one in Hungary would have dared dream of owning a car. Shops and department stores were everywhere. American capitalism was plentiful unlike the stark, barren existence under communist rule. The architecture was amazingly different than any we had seen. The snows of the Upper Peninsula were both awesome and exhausting. We hadn't seen so much snow in all our lives. I had never been a fan of the flaky little ice crystals, and I'm still not. Lake effect snow off Lake Superior has to be experienced to be believed. We were overwhelmed by the snowfalls starting in late September and lasting into May. My parents, suspicious of the huge snowfalls, even checked our latitude on a map to see how close we had come in our travels to the Arctic Circle. Local U.P. residents didn't seem to think much of the snow. It all seemed ordinary to them.

Linked to my first impressions of the U.S. and our new lives during this time are the cars of the 50s. In my mind's eye, I can still see and hear them running around on tire chains, which were a necessity for getting through the drifting snows on the streets and highways of the U.P. The cars of the 50s were, and still remain for me the best that Detroit ever produced. The late 50s offered cars that were two toned, chrome, and tail finned marvels. Detroit would never do better than this. What came off the assembly lines of General Motors, Chrysler, and Ford in these days, were masterpieces in automobile design. The Buicks, Oldsmobiles, Pontiacs, and Cadillacs of this time period moved down the streets like miniature tanks. I developed an obsession with identifying cars in these days. I even made a competition out of it with my brother Joe. I would wager that I could identify a car more quickly and accurately than he could. We would spot a car in the distance, make our best guess of make and model, and then if we guessed differently, run to see which one of us might be right. My dad bought a 1950 Mercury about a year after we arrived in the States. We would sit in front on the wide bench seat as he drove down highway 41, and we would try to guess the make and model of cars that moved with us or those coming head on with us. If there was a dispute about who was right, my dad would act as referee. The problem was that my brother and I knew the cars better than he did.

The years of the 50s were great times culturally in this country and these amazing cars were a reflection of that greatness. The thick heavy gauge metal gave these automobiles an authentic indestructibility. The plush interior upholstery inside killed road noise almost completely. The warmth they generated inside protected us from the cold U.P. winters. You could feel the massive weight of these cars as they glided over the road. They moved along in soft muffled comfort as if they were moving on air.

The Rotary Club put us into a temporary living situation on Fourth Street. It would be a short term placement until my father could find a job and pay for a place of our own. The interim home we were given to live in was beautiful. The Goodney family, who owned it, had moved out just recently. The house would eventually be moved from the lot, in short order, to make room for the construction of a middle school. We would only have the house until the thaw of spring when it became time for work to begin on the school.

My father got a job as a mechanic at a local garage. The owner of the garage didn't really need a mechanic, but since the Rotary club agreed to pay my father's salary, the garage owner agreed to take my father on as an employee. At this point we started renting a home on Barnum Street across the street from the Carnegie Library. We would supplement our learning of the English language with the use of the library. The librarians were a great help. Then the money coming from the Rotary club dried up. Consequently, the job with the garage did as well. The economy in the area was poor. My dad moved from one temporary job to another. These were the last years of the Eisenhower administration. Jobs became scarce in this mining area of the Upper Peninsula. And this community expected a baker to come to town, not a mechanic. The only open job in town, at the bakery, would stay open with no takers. My father bounced around doing odd jobs and finding himself out of work more often than not. Maybe he should have learned how to make donuts.

Suhajda Family's Story One Of Courage, Faith

My mother and my father shaking hands with mayor Aho of Ishpeming Michigan

Members of the Ishpeming Michigan Rotary club included Dr. Archie Narotzky, who was the refugee chairman; Mr. Howard J. Higgins, who was Rotary president; and former Mayor of Ishpeming Mr. Emil Aho, who worked in the area of public relations. Henry Voegler acted as interpreter. Retired teacher Mrs. Voelker helped us with our English. These people worked in concert helping us with everything from learning where things were in town to helping my father find work.

My brother Joe and I were enrolled in St. John's, a private catholic grade school. My brother Les was only five years of age, and would not be enrolled in school until the next year. Mrs. Voelker came to us once a week and tutored us in English. It didn't seem fair to me that our parents were in the same class with us. But then, we were all at the same level. Sorry about the "Seinfeld" reference, I couldn't help myself.

Some debate ensued amongst school administrators at St. John's, about whether my brother and I should be placed in the same grades that we attended in Hungary. Joe had been in the fourth grade, and I had just started second. We already missed more than two months of this school year because of our journey. School administrators decided Joe would stay in the fourth grade. But the next year, when we attended a public grade school, Joe's case was under reconsideration. Language skill was probably the main hitch in the decision to be made about how Joe would proceed in his education. Language proficiency is a more critical skill at more advanced grade levels. So Joe would be made to repeat his fourth grade year. I was advanced to third grade. With a July 7 birthday, I was already a very young second grader compared to most of my classmates. I would eventually graduate high school at the age of 17. Looking back, it would have been much better for me socially, academically and even athletically had I been given one more year of development. There were no Individual Education Plans (IEP's) in these days. There were no bilingual classes either. Ours was the school of sink or swim. The Nuns were very gracious to me. The fact that we had been refugees, I'm sure qualified us for special treatment. I have no horror stories to tell concerning rulers across knuckles or buttocks. In fact, my teacher, Sister Helen Elizabeth, was a doting and kind teacher who made sure someone in the class was helping me when I experienced problems. I don't remember being scolded or disciplined. The Nuns were just alright with me. My Hungarian teacher Bagosi Néni , (Mrs. Bagosi) gave me some good basic training back in the old country. She made us toe the line. Sister Elizabeth was a light weight compared to the boot camp I already experienced in Hungary.

Me getting reading instruction

My brothers and I were amazed with everything American, including the holidays. There was no Halloween in Hungary. Christmas here in the States was at an entirely different level, in terms of giving and receiving than what we ever experienced before. And the Fourth of July celebration was simply the "bomb."

It was the lack of employment opportunities for my dad that eventually pushed my parents to move from Ishpeming. Rotary Club members urged my father to go on government assistance when he was between jobs. My parents were embarrassed by the prospect of having to do this. My father would say to us, "I didn't come to America to live off these people." Howard Higgins (a journalist in Marquette, Mich.) advised us to move where my dad could find work. There also seemed to be some dispute among Rotary members in terms of how the job situation was being handled concerning my father. Rotary people believed in private schools and "shops" that were non-union. So when it came time for my dad to become a union member at any of his jobs, the Rotary people would move him to another job. Higgins was one of the people critical of how our situation was being handled in terms of my father's employment. The last time we saw Howard Higgins, he was telling us that he was also leaving the U.P. seeking employment in far away places like Arizona and California.

By this time, we were communicating with our relatives in Hungary. My Menráth grandmother (Anna) now knew we were safe and a half a world away in America. My Suhajda grandmother (Marika) knew of a Hungarian couple in Aurora, Illinois who had relatives living in her village. The word was that job opportunities in Aurora were very good. Our Suhajda grandmother got the address and phone number of the Sánta (Shon-taw) family in Aurora, and sent the information to us in a letter. My dad made the phone contact and arranged to drive to Aurora, where he stayed with the family while he found work. Aurora was a much larger town than Ishpeming, and full of industry. It was a few weeks after my father traveled to Aurora, when he found employment, and called for us to join him. We said goodbye to friends we made, one of whom came to say their farewell to us at the train station. We boarded a train headed for Chicago singing a song that a witch doctor friend taught David Seville. It went: ooh...eeh...ooh...ah...aah......ting...tang...walla...walla...bing...bang.............. ooh...eeh...ooh...ah..ah...ting...tang...walla...walla...bang...bang. The name of the song is "The Witch Doctor." I still sing the song to my granddaughter Alyssa.

We arrived at Chicago's Union Station after a thousand verses of "The Witch Doctor" and boarded a Burlington Northern commuter headed for Aurora. It was the summer of 1958. Mr. Gábor Sánta came to pick us up from the station. We got off the train in Aurora and walked out onto South Broadway (Rt.25) and into Mr. Sánta's car for the ride to his home in the Pigeon Hill section of the East Side of Aurora. My dad had not been able to come to pick us up. He was working.

Aurora would become our new home in our new world. Coming to Aurora culminated a journey that started almost two years before. My brothers and I would grow up here in this city. The three of us would attend the public school system on the East side of Aurora, School District 131. All three of us would graduate from East Aurora High School. We grew into young adults in this community. We had wonderful teachers and many good friends. We became Americans here. We came of age. Then on May 24, 1966 my mom gave birth to our sister Marianna (Babi). After three "bad boys," she was desperate for a beautiful little girl. And she got one.

L to R: Joe Suhayda, Marianna Suhayda, Les Suhayda, Bill Suhayda

EPILOGUE

A GROWING CONCERN FOR OUR COUNTRY

America is not only the land of the free, it is also the land of the immigrant. And it is the freedoms America provides that keep immigrants coming to her shores. If you are hardworking and honest in this country, you can make it. Add to this equation an education, and an understanding that what you do with your life is more important than what government or anyone else can do for you, and you have a formula for success. However, America does not provide guarantees. There are no guarantees in life. Nor should there be. Guarantees can make us behave like Kardashians.

When we grow up, we understand that there is no Santa Claus or even an Easter Bunny. And when we grow up, we should understand that the onus is on every one of us to work for what we want in life. Work is what gives meaning to our lives. This is why unemployment and welfare can be so demoralizing for our citizens. I tried to teach these things to my students and athletes for 34 years of my life. Unfortunately, too many Americans are not learning these important lessons today. Immigrants to this country understand these things intuitively.

I learned some important lessons in my years as an educator and coach. We teachers are always learning right along with our students. One of the most enlightening lessons I learned as a coach was that those athletes of mine who had early successes, sometimes didn't have as much success later. Those athletes who struggled early, and didn't quit, were often the ones who went on to have more success later, even in their private lives. When we learn to work, and that work leads to success, we learn its value. But if success comes too easily, and with little effort, it is much harder to consider it worthy.

My coaches used to tell me that victory is 5 percent inspiration and 95 percent perspiration. I believe this is one of the reasons immigrants do so well in our country. Immigrants who escaped controlling regimes, have worked hard to overcome adversity and the despots who controlled their lives. When they come to the U.S., they realize that they work for themselves--not the collective. These people come to the realization that government here doesn't take what they have worked to own or most of what they earn. Their work doesn't go to enrich the socialist collective, it enriches them and their families more. This incentivizes work.

Unfortunately, this is changing in our country today. Our government has grown programs that redistribute our wealth. Those people on the receiving end of this shift in wealth can become complacent and even dependent on government as a result. They start to look to government for solutions to their problems, and not to themselves. Our government is becoming bloated with social programs. These programs are becoming increasingly more expensive and even burdensome for taxpayers to support. Our national debt is at the brink of $20 trillion today. It doubled in just the last seven years. The tax burden is becoming a deterrent for our citizens to working harder. It is also chasing our industry from the country. Why stay or work harder when the more you make, the more they take? We are becoming a poorer country because work is no longer encouraged as it used to be. Our industry leaves us for tax relief.

We need to continue to remember why this country became the most prosperous country in the world. We need to remember what made this nation great. The answer to both of these questions is the same. It has been because of our limitations on big, controlling government. Government takes away the fuel that runs an economy. And it takes away our incentives to work hard. It takes away people's money that they purchase with, and with which they invest and determine the fate of their families.

Kobe Bryant puts asses into seats. The Lakers like that, and pay him accordingly. A CEO of a company, who makes the stockholders happy and their corporations prosperous, should get the same treatment. In a free enterprise system, it is the market that determines the value of our work, not the government. If we as individuals understand that, we will better ourselves to the point that we make ourselves marketable. In turn, the country does better because wealth is being created, not just redistributed. Shifting the same weights around on the pan of a scale does not change the balance of the scale. And so it follows that shifting money from one pocket to another doesn't make us more wealthy as a country. Creating a building, or a car, or any of the things that manufacturing companies make does increase the wealth of our people. It is time that we stop demonizing those in our country who produce our jobs and become prosperous in that process.

Vladimir Lenin ushered in communism to the USSR by demonizing those who owned property and produced jobs and wealth. It is, after all, easy to convince any populace of the demonic nature of the rich. This anger, on the part of the proletariat, in Russia provided kindling to ignite the Bolshevik revolution. Then, once Lenin was successful in taking all of the wealth from the wealthy by nationalizing it, the people of Russia got even poorer. This happened until 1989, when the USSR finally collapsed under the sheer weight of a totalitarian government that not only bankrupted itself, but also murdered at least 60 million people in Russia and Eastern Europe in that process.

I've had the unfortunate occasion in my life to see how people live in a huge controlling totalitarian state. I've had the good fortune to compare that with a system of government that allowed it's people the freedom to be creative and as a result prosperous here in the U.S. It is our constitution that has kept government at bay, and out of the American people's lives so that they could act in their own best interest and not the government's. Our Constitution is designed to limit the power of government over the people. It was originally designed to prevent a king or a Stalin from ruling over us, and taking our wealth and our freedoms. As long as our electorate continues to put people into the most powerful positions in our government who respect our Constitution, our way of life, and our rights, we will do fine.

But will our people continue to value our free enterprise system, our civil liberties, and our traditions. How will we continue to choose between free enterprise and government intrusion into our lives and into our economy? The framers of this nation put its people in control of all this. Let's make sure we keep that control for our sake. Those of us who have come to this country from communism realize how valuable freedom is. We also realize how very easily it can be lost.

BIOGRAPHIES AND OTHER SHORT STORIES

Rudi Rothenfelder

Born: circa 1913
Germany
Died: circa 1990
Germany

I haven't mentioned Rudi in any part of this book to this point. I mention him now, because he was such an important figure in my parent's survival and subsequent wedding at the very end of World War II. So without Rudi, the story you just read may never have been written. I don't know exactly when Rudi was born or in what city of Germany...but I think it to be a very accurate guess that he was born in Germany. Where or when he died is also an unknown to me at this point. However, it became evident in the mid-nineties that Rudi had already passed on. My parents attended a reunion of Hungarian, German, and even American aviators of World War II in Budapest in '94. Rudi was conspicuously absent. Then, through contacts made to Rudi's brother, it was learned that Rudi had passed a few years before.

Rudi had been one of the commanding officers of the flight squadron in which my father served in the Hungarian Air Force. He was a German officer and a former fighter pilot in the Luftwaffe. The events that brought Rudi to this assignment in Hungary are, in themselves, amazing. He was transferred from the Luftwaffe in Germany to this Air Force unit in Székesfehérvár, Hungary. Rudi had been shot down, over the Mediterranean Sea, near Greece by an American pilot in 1941. Interestingly, Rudi had shot the American aviator down simultaneously in a head on attack waged by both pilots. The American had been flying a P-38. ...Rudy an Me-109.

The two men parachuted into the waters of the Mediterranean Sea within sight of each other. Once in the water, the American realized that his floatation device had been shot through and wouldn't hold adequate air pressure to keep him afloat. He had also suffered bullet wounds in the air battle. They were not yet life threatening at this point. Rudi also suffered injuries in the exchange of machine gun fire, but was not seriously injured. Unlike the American, he was successful in inflating his small raft. Then when he looked up to see where his adversary might be, he realized the American was in trouble. He paddled his small "dingy" in the direction of the floundering American pilot. As he got closer, Rudi noticed the seriousness of the predicament this former combatant was in. There was blood floating on top of the choppy waves and as a result of his injuries, the man was having some difficulty treading water. Not having a functioning life raft would most certainly result in this man's death, Rudi thought.

The two men were quiet at first. They looked at each other dumbfounded in the strange predicament. Neither was sure what would or should happen next. Neither could understand what the other said. It seemed to Rudi that the hostilities had come to their natural end. He had a decision to make about whether to leave the American in what would become his watery grave.....or pull him to the safety of his own life raft. Rudi chose plan B.

Minutes before, they were pitted against each other in a life or death struggle. Now he was saving this man's life. The air battle between the two men had never been personal of course. They were like two wrestlers pitted against one another in competition. Rudi understood the rules had now changed. It was the sight of this man's face..... and seeing him in mortal danger that had made them different.

The Mediterranean is, of course, a big body of water. To this point, both aviators escaped each other's attempts at killing one another. Now their lives would depend on each other's cooperation before they could be plucked from the sea. The American now made his contribution to the survival effort with a yellow dye that he released into the water to make it easier for search planes and ships to spot them. Within just 24 hours they were rescued by a Greek merchant vessel and taken to a hospital somewhere in Greece.

The two injured pilots were placed into beds next to each other. During their convalescence, they had interpreters who aided them in their communication. The American Red Cross supplied the hospital with all of the medication and supplies necessary for the American pilot's recovery. The hospital purposefully kept the American for longer than was necessary. The longer they kept the American, the more health supplies the hospital received from the American Red Cross. The two men even left the hospital and enjoyed each others company over a glass or two of Ouzo (oozo). On the day that they were discharged from the hospital, they embraced each other as friends.

Fast forward to 1944. Adolf Hitler, a madman, has already assassinated most of his military leaders including Erwin Rommel. His replacement troops, for a devastated infantry, are made up mostly of "Hitler Youth" who, in many cases, are only fifteen years of age. It was common knowledge to most, with the likely exception of the Fuhrer, that the war was lost. Hungary had wanted out of the war even before Hitler's unsuccessful assassination attempt in '44. Hitler sensed that Miklós Hórthy, the

Hungarian Prime Minister at this time, was losing his enthusiasm for the war effort. Hitler had the Prime Minister's son kidnapped for safe keeping, to ensure Hungary stayed in the conflict. The young Hórthy became an insurance policy for Hitler, to make sure that the Prime Minister kept his troops in the war. Hitler would later depose Hórthy and insert his own puppet government. As a result, Hungary would stay in the war until its bitter end.

My parents had been engaged by '43, although for a while, that fact had been kept secret from my grandparents. My father developed a "friendly" relationship with Rudi and my mom got to know him on those social occasions when my dad met with his commanding officer socially. The fact she was fluent in German, certainly helped in this relationship. Many of the pilots in my father's squadron were being lost in this now, lost war. Of course my mom feared for the life of her fiance in this now lost cause. So unbeknownst to my father, Irén went to Rudi to make a very delicate but dangerous request. She asked that Rudi not send my father into battle. Rudi was astonished by the request and even angered, but he took the time to tell my mom why her request was improper and that it could even land him in front of a firing squad. Doing what Irén requested would be considered an act of treason in the eye's of his superiors.

And then came a very fateful day. On a routine training mission, my father (Lajos), lost one of his main landing gears during take-off. The Me-109 ground looped flipping onto its back. Fuel dripped from the tanks of the plane as Lajos tried to free himself from his shoulder harness in this very awkward upside down position. To limit the possibility of fire, my father already shut off the master switch to the electronics on the airplane, a standard part of crash procedure. Any short circuit eliciting sparks would ignite the expanding gasoline vapors, and could instantly turn this crash sight into an inferno. The ground crew, rushing to my father's rescue, brought pick axes with which to chop holes in the fuselage, through which they planned to extricate him from the crumpled plane. They obviously were not considering that this kind of metal on metal contact would likely create sparks. Some of the strikes with the pick axes came close to my father's body. He yelled out to stop trying to save him so aggressively. Those may not have been his exact words, however. He related this story to me during the time I was a student pilot at Aurora Municipal Airport some 30 years later. Lajos stressed the importance of shutting off the master switch during a crash to prevent fires. He also told me how lucky he felt surviving the pickaxes of his very clumsy but well intentioned saviors.

Rudi had an investigation done to determine the cause of the accident. Not much investigating had to be done, however, since the separated main gear of the aircraft was a quarter mile away from where the main wreckage of the airplane came to rest. The cause of the crash was self evident. It was a mechanical failure due to overuse and under maintanance of these airplanes. These planes, it seemed, didn't roll down the runway well without two healthy and attached main gears.

Rudi's memory went back to my mom's emotional request to keep my father out of the war. He now saw a way in which he could accomplish what my mom had been asking for. He would "deep six" this report on the official reasons for the crash, and declare this incident to be a result of pilot error. Pilot error was grounds for disqualifying an airman from combat duty. My father would not be sent into battle for the rest of the war.

It was April of 1945 and the waning days of World War II. The U.S. and Great Britain attacked Germany and the Axis countries from the West. Russia attacked from the East. Being much closer in proximity to Russia than to the Western Allied forces, Hungary was overrun by the Red Army. This became the beginning of the occupation of Hungary by the Soviet Union. Up to this point, the reputation of Russian Soldiers to murder, rape, and commit acts of debauchery had been infamous throughout the world. They did not disappoint now. As they rolled into Hungary and other Eastern European countries, they decimated everything and every person in their wake. A huge portion of Eastern Europe fell under Stalin's boot.

The leadership of Lajos' squadron decided that they were not going to surrender anything or anyone to the Russians. This squadron of planes and support personnel would move west to Austria and then Germany to surrender to the Americans, never to the Russians. My parents' wedding had been scheduled for the day after this movement of soldiers, pilots, and planes started. My father asked his superior officer if he could stay behind for just one day to be married. His request was denied. But because my father had documentation of the fact that a wedding had been planned, his commanding officer indicated that he would allow my mom to leave with the squadron in their exodus from the country. Lajos made a phone call to the post office in Rábakecskéd. It was the town closest to where Irén and my grandparents lived in Börgönd.[15] The message simply stated that Irén should join him as soon as she could. The movement of planes, equipment and personnel had already started. My father was in Csapod, a town already close to the Austrian border. My grandparents encouraged my mom to go with the squadron at this point, knowing what might very well happen to a young attractive woman during the Russian invasion and subsequent occupation. But how was Irén going to get to where Lajos was? There was a German battalion of soldiers in the vicinity also headed west for Germany. They would be leaving shortly before the arrival of the Red Army. They were headed in the direction of Csapod. My mom went to the commander of the German battalion and asked if she could go with them. She explained her reasons and the location of my father's unit. As it turned out, the battalion would be approximately in the same places as the Air squadron. It worked out that my mom was able to join up with Lajos in Csapod, close to Sopron in the Northwest corner of the country.

The airplanes were flown out at a hundred or so kilometers at a time. The rest of the convoy would then catch up with them. They "puddle jumped" like this until they got into Austria. Then in Fraam Austria, just

---

15 *The only places people could receive phone calls in these days were at post offices. A messenger would be sent out into the village to retrieve the person getting a phone call. If the person could not be found immediately, a message would be taken and delivered later. This was before anyone in Hungary would have a phone in their home.*

a short distance from St. Pölten, the airplanes were destroyed in an Allied air attack as they sat on the ground. The company moved along by trucks and the personnel carriers that were still operational, from then on. The squadron eventually reached Poking Germany, where they surrendered to American forces.

My parents were married on April 26, 1945 in a school house next to a bombed out church in Schönburg, Germany. They would spend the first six months of their marriage segregated from each other in a prisoner of war camp in nearby Poking. Then in October, they were released and shipped back to Hungary. The Americans and the American leadership treated all prisoners of war with respect and care.[16] They developed a roster of names of those prisoners they had had in the POW camp.

This group of people were then kept track of by the Americans to make sure they were not mistreated or imprisoned by the Russians upon their return to Hungary. My parents were grateful for the good treatment they received.[17] They mentioned this fact to us many times over the years.

16 *I'm sure one of the reasons that we came to these United States had to do with the fact my parents had a high regard for Americans and America. And this gratitude they developed for America, had everything to do with this humane treatment they received as POWs in Poking.*

17 *My Dad already earned the good treatment of Americans by this time, even if the Americans didn't know it. Towards the end of the war, a squadron of American B-24's were doing a bombing run in the area around Székesfehérvár, where my father was stationed in the Hungarian Air Force. It would have been standard procedure for my father and the other pilots in his unit to take off and get all of the airplanes airborne to do battle, or simply prevent the airplanes from being destroyed on the ground in the air raid. But by this time in the war, there were fuel shortages in Hungary and fuel was not available on this day to get the planes off the ground. One of the B-24's had been hit by ground to air fire and was in a shallow dive as all of the airman in the bomber hit the "silk" (parachutes). All of the pilots in my dad's squadron went in the direction of the Americans parachuting to the ground. My dad came upon an American who was already on the ground. Locals from a nearby village were on the scene and looking as if they were about to kill the man with pitchforks, hatchets, or anything else they brought with them. My dad pulled his service revolver and put it at his side as he approached and commanded the locals to disperse and go back home. The American on the ground was already gravely injured but not by the actions of the locals. He suffered shrapnel wounds to his torso. The American clutched at the crucifix he had on a necklace softly saying "mother," "mother." My dad understood what it was the American was*

(cont. on next page.)

In contrast, Hungarians who were captured by the Russians were sent to labor camps in Russia and Siberia. Many of them were never heard from again. Many young women were taken from their families and sent to these horrific labor camps. Those who survived came back skin and bones, and in some cases pregnant as a result of the rapes they endured. Bones that broke were not set properly. There was little to no medical care for POWs in Russia. The arms and legs of these unfortunate people curved off at strange angles. They suffered from parasites and malnourishment. Their faces were sunken and skeletal. Many lost their teeth. These were young men and women before they were taken. Now they looked decades beyond their chronological age, their health broken. It was a very good thing that my mother had the good fortune to be able to follow my father, and be with him in an American POW camp. So if it hadn't been for Rudi Rothenfelder, it is very possible that neither of my parents would have survived the war.

---

trying to communicate. It was obvious to my father that the man was dying and he didn't want this necklace taken from him by my dad or anyone else. My father guessed the necklace was probably a gift from the man's mother. Perhaps it had been a good luck charm. My dad asked for someone in the group of villagers to get a doctor. My dad stayed with the American and tried to comfort him until medical attention arrived. My father never found out if the American aviator survived. But he did his best to preserve this man's life and to keep his crucifix around his neck.

I visited the Aurora Airport aviation museum a few months back. In looking at the artifacts of World War II memorabilia on display, I saw a letter from a high ranking U.S. Air Force officer addressed to the parents of an airman in New Jersey who bailed out of a B24. The letter explained the airman had been attacked by locals and injured severely in an area in Hungary very close to where my father was stationed in Székesfehérvár. After talking with my Mom about the exact location where my father had had this encounter, we decided that the airman being referred to in the letter, was more than likely not the same man my father found severely injured. It was however, a very eerie letter to read.

Rudi Rothenfelder

BIOGRAPHIES AND OTHER SHORT STORIES

Menráth Irén
(Ee-rain) Suhayda

Born: Versec, Yugoslavia
April 29, 1928

My mother is a practical, intelligent, and discriminating woman. I've always known her to be inquisitive about anything and everything. As I was growing up, if she didn't know the answer to something, she would look it up in the library of encyclopedias she purchased just for this purpose. Brenda, my wife, still talks about how she remembers my mom paging through her "Britannicas," looking for tidbits of information on topics for which she wanted more clarity. She still finds great joy in googling for information at age 88. She is a person of culture without being pretentious. Social graces and etiquette have always been of importance to her. Proper dress and the recognition of social customs were high on her list of good and proper character traits. Having civility and being cultured were stressed in our home. For my mother, being your best self, at all times, remained a high priority.

Without her, my father's life would have been an organizational mess. I'm convinced he would not have lived much past 70 had it not been for my mother's meticulous care. My father was diagnosed with diabetes at 65. It was because of my mother's attention to detail, and her strict adherence to a disciplined insulin regimen that he would live to 91. My dad was as much of a dreamer as my mom was a pragmatist. They were polar opposites in many respects. Where my father saw opportunity, my mom saw risk. Where my father saw adventure, my mom saw danger. Where my father saw white, my mom saw black. But there were obviously some things they collaborated on seeing as they brought four children into the world.

My mother always regretted the fact that she didn't complete a formal education. The fact is, she didn't have the opportunity to even finish high school. The "schooling" she received, was in my estimation, much more valuable than the type that we shell out tens of thousands of dollars for these days. That tuition price tag may very well be in the six-figure range by now. A little thing called World War II played a significant role in preventing my mom from finishing her education. The other piece had to do with a father who worked for the railroad, and kept getting transferred from one railroad station to another on a regular basis. Where there were problems, my grandfather was sent to fix them. For most women in Europe during this time, there wasn't a high priority to become educated. My grandfather's relocations even involved moves to other countries. My mom was very adaptive, and she learned new languages in the process of these moves. By the time her pre-teen years rolled around, she spoke three languages. But the constant change did eventually end her ability to stay in school. Her academics had been short-circuited, but her understanding of cultures and languages became very well developed.

Menráth Mátyás and Menráth Ana Bittlingmayer, my mom's parents, as you may discern from their names, were of German descent. All of the people on my mother's side are of that heritage going back as many generations as we can follow. As a result, my mom's first language was German. Then when she went to school in the former Yugoslavia, she learned Serbian. The First World War produced hatred between the people of Yugoslavia and Germany. The simple fact my grandparents were Germans living in Yugoslavia brought a certain amount of disfavor. Because of the persecution of Germans in Yugoslavia, my grandfather Mátyás moved the family to Hungary. He no longer considered Yugoslavia a safe place for his family. So Hungarian became my mother's third language. Upon immigrating to the U.S. in 1957, English became my mother's fourth language at age 28. She continues to speak English to this day, and quite well.

My mom and my grandparents led both interesting and dangerous lives during World War Two. For a while, they lived on the second floor of a train depot my grandfather managed. Railroads were the major supply lines by which things moved from place to place in Europe during this time period. The military effort of the Axis powers in Europe relied on these rail routes for the production and resupplying of war machinery, and even the movement of troops. Everything from food to armaments traveled by rail. There was also the trafficking of human cargo in the form of Jewish people shipped from all parts of Europe to the concentration camps in Germany and Poland. Many of these people moved through my grandfather's train depot. Railways became strategic targets to be bombed and destroyed in order to disrupt the supply lines of war. My grandparents and mom ended up in the middle of many air attacks, especially in the waning period of the war.

A certain level of complacency started to set in with my mom in this regard. Since she no longer attended school, my grandfather put her to work for him in his station's telegraph / post office. She took in mail, issued stamps, and did bookkeeping, filing and other clerical work. On one particular day, as had occurred on several others, the air raid sirens sounded as she tended to a line of customers at her window. Other than quickening her pace, she showed no indication of closing down her customer line. She was not heading for the air raid shelter, although my grandfather already told her to close down and proceed in that direction. Her customers showed no signs of wanting to move for cover either. Perhaps they took their cues from this cool and collected young woman. Perhaps they didn't want to lose their place in line. Irén worked quickly to serve as many people as she could before heading for safety. She wanted to get as much work done as she could before leaving her post. But she had waited too long. The American fighters made up of one P-38 and three P-51's, were on their way. All of the chickens in the yards of the village had gone into their coups a long time ago. The chickens were great at telling people of impending air raids. They headed for shelter long before any sirens went off. So if you wanted advance warning of these attacks, you didn't wait for air raid sirens, you watched the behavior of these fowl.

Everyone in town heard the airplanes by now as these customers looked to find a safe place to hide. My mom headed for the air raid shelter outside the building in an underground bunker. The door to the bunker slanted at a 45-degree angle to the ground. In order to get into the enclosure, you had to step down a few steps, and then pull the door on top of you until gravity did its work to close it for you. There were four airplanes maneuvering themselves into a flight pattern for the attack. My grandfather had the thick, heavy gauge metal door open for his daughter as he watched the first P-38 in a dive coming towards the station. He yelled for his daughter to run as fast as she could. My mom heard but could not see the plane behind her as she ran for the shelter. She now understood her silly mistake at having been too intent on serving her customers, and realized the grave danger she had created for herself. My grandfather grabbed her arm to pull her in, as he closed the steel door all in one motion. Bullets from six .50 caliber machine guns of the fighter plane's cannons bounced off the metal door as it closed. She cheated death, but only by the narrowest of margins.

Another fortunate soul who waited too long to find cover stood in the crotch of a tree with twin trunks. The trunks of the tree were in line with the direction of the assault and served to protect him perfectly from the attacks that alternately came from one side of the station, and then the other. But the tree hadn't protected one of the legs of his trousers from being "skewered." One bullet pierced his pant leg, narrowly missing his shin.

There was another day on which a train full of Italian Jews came through the station. My mom looked on in horror to see these people crammed into cattle cars so tightly they couldn't sit down. There was one young woman who managed to find a resting place however. She sat in the doorway of the cattle car dangling her legs just a foot or two from the rocks next to the tracks. In her arms was her 2-year-old child. She was a beautiful child with dark hair, and dark sad eyes. The mother gestured to Irén by bringing her hand to her mouth as a person would when taking a bite of food. Irén understood immediately what the woman was trying to communicate, but she didn't think she had the time to go upstairs to her kitchen before the train pulled out of the station. So Irén quickly went to an elderly woman sitting in front of the depot on a bench and asked if she might have something for this poor unfortunate woman. The elderly lady reached into her bag and apologetically offered Irén a small red apple. "This is all I have," she said. Irén took the apple and went to the train car to give this small morsel of food to the hungry woman and her child. The woman looked at Irén and the elderly woman with gratitude as she gave the apple to her little girl. There were tears in the woman's eyes as the little girl took her first bite. Incredibly, some of the adults around the woman reached for the apple now in the hand of the child. The mother fended off the "starving" hands allowing her child to consume this small bit of food.

An S.S. officer came running, yelling and pointing his rifle at Irén asking her in German what she thought she was doing. Irén understood him perfectly of course and answered back in German telling him her disgust with how these people were being treated. The officer, surprised to hear this young woman speaking in perfect German, calmed himself and answered back, "These are not people, they are Jews." Irén replied, "To me, they are people." The soldier, now angered by Irén's response to him, threatened to throw both Irén and the elderly lady, who offered the apple, into the cattle car with these poor unfortunates. But before he could act, the train lunged forward. The soldier retreated, and hopped back onto the moving train.

My mother revealed many disturbing stories to us concerning this time period in history. She saw and experienced some horrible things in her lifetime. But of all the horrible scenes she has told me about, this one has always been the most memorable and horrible one for me. It is especially horrible because of what we now know, concerning where these people were headed. Hope can keep us safe from thinking the worst, but it is difficult to remain hopeful about what the eventual fate was for this mother and child, knowing what we know of the Holocaust.

I think because of my mom's life experiences, she has always been a woman of humility. She suffered in her life, especially as a result of being separated from family. But she has never allowed adversity to destroy her spirit or her pride in self. The difficulties my mom experienced in life has revealed her strong character.

My childhood memories of my mother do not include many soft and cuddly moments. I always understood however, that she loved us all dearly, but it was a tough love, with high expectations for character and accomplishment. I believe she got what she aimed for.

Menráth Irén Suhayda

BIOGRAPHIES AND OTHER SHORT STORIES

Suhayda Lajos (Law-Yosh) Zoltán (Zoli)

Born: Battonya, Hungary
  June 19, 1919
Died: Komló, Hungary
  Sept. 6, 2010

My father was studying the science of flight in the days when most others were riding around in horse drawn carriages. If there were any paper airplanes flying around in his classrooms at school, he was probably the perpetrator, although his purposes for launching them would likely have been for testing his most recent engineering design, rather than for reasons of mischief. But I could be wrong. Zoli, as he was known in his hometown, was building model airplanes a mere three decades after the Wright brothers had recorded their first powered flight in 1903.

World War I ended seven months before my father was born. The war had been a disaster for the Austrian/Hungarian Empire. Hungary lost two thirds of her territory, and as a result of the loss of that territory, half of her population at the conclusion of the war. The borders were redrawn as a result of a "treaty" called Trianon. Hungarians, including my maternal grandparents, found themselves in different countries without even leaving their homes. But as disastrous as the war had been for everyone concerned, it had been a boon to aviation. Incorporating aviation into military strategy put the science of flight on the front burners of the technology of the time. The battle for air superiority between countries escalated the science and design of flying machines.

"If God had intended for man to fly, He would have given him wings." God didn't give my father wings, but the Hungarian Air force would, he thought. Young Zoli understood that the only way he would ever have a chance to fly was through military service; however, his path to getting into aviation would not be that easy or direct. When young Zoli reached the critical age at which he could volunteer for military service, he enlisted into the Air Force. This was his first mistake. To my father's dismay, the Air Force would not give him the wings he desired via the enlistment route. To get into the cockpit of an airplane, you had to be accepted and enrolled into the flight training academy of the country. The path he set out on would only guarantee to put a wrench, an oil can, or a gas nozzle in his hand, not the controls of an airplane.

As soon as he learned of his mistake, Zoli went to his commanding officer and asked for a transfer to the flight school in Szombathely for flight training. His commander told young Zoli, (now referred to by his legal first name Lajos...Law-yos, Louis) to "stop dreaming." But dreaming is what my father did best, even when awake. So when he received "leave time" he traveled to Budapest to speak to none other than the Secretary of the Air Force. In vintage Lajos style, he was flying right over the head of his commanding officer - a more dangerous maneuver than the outside loop.

My father was never a patient man, especially when he wanted something. It was very much in his nature to circumvent any chain of command blocking his way. When a decision needed to be made, he went straight to the source of decision-making power. When my father made up his mind about doing something, it was going to happen. This was one of his great strengths, and also a trait that landed him in the most trouble.

My father didn't see obstacles, he saw solutions. Nothing was impossible. It was my mom who tended to the details of starting at point "A" and getting to destination"B." She was the one who saw the hurdles to be navigated and the particulars to be considered. So my mom rarely deemed the dreamer side of my father to be a good thing. She saw the risks that my father would take as sources of frustration as well as economic commitments she didn't think we could afford. My Mom was usually under some stress as a result of having three boys to tend too, a house to keep up, a full-time job, and managing the household budget. My father would tell my mother about his dreams. My mother would tell him why they were not possible. Both my parents were stubborn to a fault. But in a war of wills, my father almost always came up the winner. My father lived very much by impulse. My mom lived by the dread of the consequences of those impulses.

Young Lajos managed to get an appointment with the Secretary of the Air Force while on leave in Budapest. How he managed that feat remains a mystery. But even more amazingly, my father convinced the Secretary to give him the transfer that his commanding officer denied him. Young Lajos would become a pilot--and not just any kind of pilot. He would become a fighter pilot in the Hungarian Air Force, flying one of the most advanced fighter planes of World War II, the Messerschmitt--also known as the ME-109.

My father had aspirations of getting into aviation in the U.S. after having had "political" problems in that industry back in Hungary. But for at least a couple of reasons, he would be unsuccessful in getting back into flying. First, the communist government that we had escaped held all of my father's log books, and that government considered those records as government property. My father had no independent records of what he did in the Air Force during his military career. He couldn't prove anything about his experience in aviation. Secondly, my father never was able to learn the English language proficiently enough to make flying his profession. He was already 38 years of age when we came to the States, and he had very limited English skills. His window of opportunity for learning the English language, or any language for that matter, closed a long time ago. It took him 20 years before he would even be able to pass the written exam to become a private pilot. But when he did, he and I became co-owners of a PA-22 Piper Tri-pacer.

We would become co-owners of a second airplane (a PA-28 Cherokee 140) after he flipped the Tri-pacer onto its back in a stiff crosswind landing. The airplane was a total loss. Old Louie walked away from the wreckage with only a sore back. This was his second plane crash, while pilot in command, that he had walked away from. The first one was on take off in an ME-109. He lost a main gear on take off and ground looped the airplane in that crash. Ironically, it was his ground crew that almost killed him with pickaxes while trying to extricate him from the crumpled airplane and not the crash itself.

My father swore he would never go back to live in Hungary as long as there was a communist form of government running the country. But when we were given amnesty from that government for our illegal escape, we did go back to visit relatives. My father went back for a visit in 1974... alone. He went back to the small town of Dombegyház in which he grew up. Old Louis had developed a kind of celebrity in this small agricultural community. After all, not too many people of this village had become fighter pilots. And there probably weren't any former residents of this small town who had escaped during the revolution or for that matter resided in the United States. During his flight training in Szeged, young Louie had the eccentric habit of "dropping off" his dirty laundry into his family's back yard. The eccentric part of this had to do with the fact that he would do this "dropping off" from the cockpit of an airplane as he buzzed the neighborhood from an altitude of 50 feet. He was literally dive bombing his parents' home with dirty underwear. These stunts made him into a legendary figure in his village.

Old Louis came back home wanting to flaunt his celebrity status with his relatives and friends just a bit and decided to throw a dinner party at a local Restaurant. He invited a good portion of the town to the eating house where he wined and dined relatives, friends and new acquaintances. What came next became a bit of folklore history in the town and among our relatives as well. It remains, in my mind, one of the ballsiest..... in your face moves I've ever heard done. Old Louis had brought back to this communist country small American flags that he placed on each table in the restaurant as the dinner was being served. Mind you, that at this point in history, the Cold War was still in full force. Leonid Brezhnev was the General Secretary of the communist party in the Soviet Union. In attendance at the dinner party was the local chief of police. My father could very easily have been arrested for doing what he had just done. What eventually did happen was that he was banned from ever entering the country again. My father would have the last laugh, however. He outlived this communist regime that we escaped, which now also made this judgement against him. He moved back to Hungary, and once more, lived as a free man in this the country of his birth.

What my father was thinking when he pulled this stunt, I would never know for sure. But knowing him as I did, I would assume that this was an "in your face" [18]moment that he had planned for no other reason than that

---

18 *I visited my father for the last time in his life in the summer of 2010. My wife Brenda and I stopped in Budapest for a couple of nights on our way back home, before getting on our plane, to enjoy this beautiful historic city and its architecture and restaurants for the last couple of days of our trip. We took a dinner cruise on the Danube in the downtown area, and the vicinity of the Parliament building where the fateful shot was fired by an AVO (SS) guard to spark the revolt of 1956. We floated peacefully, sipping a white zinfandel, past the*

(cont. on next page.)

he was angered by this regime. It was something he never discussed with me or anyone else in our immediate family except perhaps my mom. It is

---

spot that was the sight of unbelievable carnage just a little over a half century before.

We enjoyed chicken paprikás and the beauty of the city lights while treated to a history lesson of this country extending back to the Roman period. The lengthy and detailed history included every conflict that ever occurred in this region going back to a period before Hungary was officially a nation. But there had been a glaring omission in the presentation. The 1956 Revolution had been edited out in total. For the uninitiated tourist, it would not have been evident that anything was missed. It was, however, very apparent to me or anyone else who knew anything about Eastern European History. Our tour guide deleted everything from this history lesson starting at the end of the second world war to the "change in government" here in 1989. It seemed as if there was no worthy history to report between 1945 and 1989. This had not been a rewriting of history....it had been an unwriting of history. And there was not a word uttered about 1956 by our tour guide "historian." Things that happened a thousand years ago had been deemed important enough to be reported, but not an event that resulted in 3,000 dead in this city alone just a little over 50 years ago. Russian tanks blew up entire city blocks, killing innocent civilians in the collapsing ruble. The omission was more than glaring, and I was infuriated.

I waited for this P.C. history lesson to end and then approached our somewhat rotund, middle aged, communist sympathizer historian tour guide. I asked him point blank and in our native tongue why he had not mentioned what happened here at the Parliament building just 54 years ago. I continued my verbal attack by asking him how he could leave out of his presentation the events that had caused 200,000 Hungarians, including my family and I, to leave this country during that time? How could he leave out an event that took the lives of thousands of people, most of whom were citizens of this city?

Unsurprisingly, I didn't get answers to my questions. All I got was a blank expression of disbelief. As I stared through this poor excuse of a historian's beady little eyes to the back of his pinheaded skull, I got the impression he never considered being called out on his edited "historical presentation." My suspicions in this regard were confirmed, when after the brief staring contest, he simply turned and walked away. I didn't pursue him or the answers to my questions any further, although I urgently wanted to. I was curious about what, if any, bluff answers he might have had. All of my questions had been rhetorical of course. Angered as I was, I at least wanted to put the guy on the spot to see what he would say. I had no need to create a bigger scene, but I did wonder what my father may have done in my position. The only satisfaction I would receive in this one sided exchange would be the knowledge that this guy knew I knew the truth about his pathetic lecture. I felt good about having stuck up for all those brave revolutionaries who fought courageously against insurmountable odds. After all, their actions made it possible for so many people to escape the repressive regime that existed here at that time. And that included me. Confronting this communist was the least I could do.

likely he thought since he was, at this point in his life, an American citizen, he was immune from arrest and prosecution for such a display. And then maybe he just didn't give a damn, and wanted to insult the local police chief and other magistrates in attendance. It certainly was an act of defiance and insult to the communist regime in power. The local police chief could have interpreted this act as an act of sedition. It could have become an international incident if he had been arrested. I first became aware of this incident from my cousin Gyuszi decades later at a time when my father was already debilitated with Parkinson's. He was no longer communicative, so I would never be able to ask him about it, or get his version of the story. I would have loved to hear his explanation of these events and his thoughts about what happened. They would certainly have been embellished in a very interesting way.

The fall of the Berlin Wall in 1989 marked the end to the USSR and communism in Europe.[19] Now my parents could move back to Hungary as free people, and they did so in 1992. They bought and owned two beautiful homes and lived very comfortably. One of the homes was located in Dombegyház, where my father grew up. The other was close to Pécs where my mom's relatives and only surviving sibling, her sister, still lived. My father would live another 19 years after his return to his homeland.

---

19 *Joe, my much older brother, and I attended a seminar at Aurora University just a few years after the Berlin wall went down in 1989. The fall of the wall had been a kind of symbol for the collapse of the Soviet Union and communism's grip on the continent. Presenting at the seminar was a "Russian Journalist." I've put "Russian Journalist" in quotes here because even our esteemed presenter considered his title to be a kind of joke when he was a "Russian Journalist." He went into some detail about what would happen to his articles when they were deemed too controversial to be published by his editor. The more critical his op-eds were of the regime, the greater the chance they would be replaced by some innocuous food recipe. He indicated that writing such articles would have resulted in imprisonment or worse just a few years before. Things had been changing in the USSR. In the Q and A that followed the presentation, I asked our "journalist's" opinion, if it was freedom of expression (the power of the pen) and a more informed Russian people (Glasnost) that brought about the downfall of the Soviet Union, rather than the arms race that Ronald Reagan had waged with the Soviet Leadership. To my surprise, his answer was an emphatic "No." He pointed at Reagan's "Star Wars" initiative and the economic burdens that that had created for the Soviet Union as the major reason for the regime's collapse.*

Communism was dead!!! He outlived them and even got the last word. There is an old saying that the greatest revenge is to live well. Compared to how we lived when we left Hungary in 1956, we lived well here in the states thanks to my parents' hard work. And when they finally went back to their beloved country, 36 years after we left it, they lived like royalty.

Suhayda Lajos Zoltán (Zoli)

In memory of my father....the Aviator

They're on opposite horizons

A vision to keep

The moon comes-a-risin'

As the sun goes to sleep

It's a reflection in darkness

And a waning of light

Colors just seen

Are removed with the night

It's a cycle an order

A rhythm a beat

The moon brings the darkness

The sun brings the heat

Beginnings and endings

Risings and settings

Crashes to Ashes

And his lust turns to dust

It's a celestial journey across a heavenly sky

His thoughts and dreams were always to fly

~ Béla

BIOGRAPHIES AND OTHER SHORT STORIES

Menráth Anna Bittlingmayer

Born: July 17, 1899
Versec Serbia
Died: April 15th, 1973
Hosszuhetény, Hungary

My grandmother was one of the hardest working people I've ever known. She worked sunrise to sunset every day that I knew her. Then, after sundown, and after the dishes were done, she would continue working into the night either knitting or doing crochet until bedtime. I pretty much lived with my grandparents between the ages of 5 and 7. I sort of considered them my parents during this time, only going home to my parents and brothers on weekends, when my father came home from his job in Komlo. Transportation to and from the mine where he worked was limited, so he stayed in a boarding house close to his work, only coming home on weekends. Omama, as we referred to her, was a very doting person, and a meticulous housekeeper. She took very good care of me and my grandfather (Mátyás) who was in failing health by this time. He died just a month before our departure from the country. One of the more dominant memories I have of my grandmother involves her skimming the fat off the surface of my grandfather's chicken soup. Many battles were fought over this unfortunate practice. Mátyás would complain strongly and would sometimes even refuse to eat the "doctored" consomme.[20] Anna explained to him the importance of watching his fat intake every time she did this. "This is for your own good" she would say. "These are doctors orders!" She was always concerned about her husband's health, and for good reason. My grandfather suffered from high blood pressure and hardening of the arteries. Both conditions contributed to his fragile and failing health. Anna kept him on as low a fat diet as she possibly could manage.

Bittlingmayer Anna was married to Menráth Mátyás at eighteen years of age. It was Mátyás' second marriage after having lost his first wife to Tuberculosis. The marriage was more an arranged marriage out of necessity than it had been about romance. The death of Mátyás first wife left him with a young boy (Menráth Lajos) to raise by himself. Mátyás was also fourteen years Anna's senior, and already well established professionally as a railroad transportation manager. Early on, the relationship was almost that of parent to child.

I missed my grandmother tremendously after our departure from the country. I didn't think we would stay in the states for long after our arrival here. In my childish imagination, I envisioned an inevitable trip back home.

---

20 *My grandfather would conspire to sneak food for him and I, when my grandmother was outside tending to the chickens or the garden. He would involve me in these clandestine adventures. My silence in these matters was rewarded with delicious slices of homemade bread. I was forbidden to have snacks too close to meal times, so this became risky business for both of us. These were deliciously secret moments I enjoyed with my grandfather. It was great fun knowing that we pulled the wool over my grandmother's eyes.*

I waited for the day my parents would tell us we were going back. I hoped for those words, but they never came. I slowly made friends with the idea that we were home here in the United States.

Then in 1966, after my sister (Babi) was born, my grandmother came on a visit and stayed more than a year helping my mom with my sister. She even came to some of my wrestling matches at East Aurora High School, even though she didn't enjoy the sport. She was still being my Omama, protective and fearful I would be hurt. I would tell her to save her concern for my opponents. She found it very odd that her frail, fair-haired little grandchild, who used to have fainting spells as a young boy, was now engaged in this grueling sport.

Then, after being here with us in the states for almost two years, my Aunt (my mom's sister Nuci), gave my mother terrible news regarding my uncle Feri (Menráth Ferdinand), who was in the hospital and close to death. My Aunt felt my grandmother should come home as quickly as possible to be with her son in his final days. He had an inoperable brain tumor and remained in a coma. Feri Bácsi, (as in Bocci ball) as we referred to him, developed this condition even before our escape from Hungary. One time, even though he had been warned by everyone not to ride a bicycle, he gave me a ride going to his house. He lost control of the two wheeler and we crashed. He had suffered a seizure, causing him to lose control of the bike. I wasn't seriously hurt, but he was profusely apologetic to my parents and I for what happened. Seeing my uncle in an uncontrollable seizure was more troubling to me than the accident.

My mom didn't tell my grandmother of the grave condition my uncle was reported to be in. She didn't want my grandmother, who also suffered from high blood pressure, to have the added stress of worrying about my uncle on the long trip home. But my mom did encourage her to go home as quickly as possible. As it turned out, my uncle passed before my grandmother even got home. The stress of her son's death took a huge toll on her. She passed away five years later, in 1973, of a massive stroke just as my grandfather had. But as a result of the special occasion of my sister's birth, I reunited with this very special woman who will forever remain one of the most important persons of my youth.

Menráth Anna Bittlingmayer

BIOGRAPHIES AND OTHER SHORT STORIES

Menráth Mátyás

Birth: June 6, 1885
Német Bencsek, Hungary...now Romania
Death: September 20th, 1956
Godisa, Hungary

I never really knew my maternal grandfather well. But that fact had nothing to do with the amount of time I spent with him in the days of my early youth. It had everything to do with the dementia from which he suffered in the last years of his life. Menráth Mátyás was a very competent manager in his day. His professional career dealt with managing railroad stations in Hungary, Romania, and Yugoslavia. In today's vernacular, he would be referred to as a troubleshooter. If there were glitches, hitches, snags, or complications to be attended to, at a station, or some kind of mismanagement, he was the one called to fix the problems. When I heard people talk about my grandfather in those early years of my young life, he was always characterized as a competent and efficient person with an attention for detail and precision. He was a man who was orderly, organized, and committed to his profession. In other words, he was a man who ran a very "tight ship."

These characteristics played out in his personal life with his family as well. He was a strict disciplinarian, with a good heart, according to my mom. He commanded respect from the people around him and from his children. As I've already described in my story here, he was a great storyteller, especially when he read to us from his magical books of mythology. He was generous with his time until fatigue took over and he fell asleep sometimes in mid sentence while reading to me. On good days, he devoted many hours to me and my brothers telling us the only stories about his life to which he had access, the stories of his youth.

Menráth Mátyáss

BIOGRAPHIES AND OTHER SHORT STORIES

Jozseph Zoltán
Suhayda

Born: May 1. 1947
Kisdombegyház, Hungary

O f the four of us siblings, Joe is the elder statesman. In our youth, he lead my younger brother and I into the uncharted waters of much mischief. He was the one entrusted with the most responsibilities by my parents. He also had the added good fortune of reaching physical maturity in the shortest span of time. He was as tall in his Freshman year in High School as he is today. My brother Les and I lagged far behind. We were in college before we reached our full physical maturity. Joe was always the boss and my brother Les and I knew it. The family pecking order was well established.[21]

21 *It had become a tradition in the Suhajda family to name the first male child of the family Joszef. My brother became the most recent recipient of this honor. This tradition had gone*

(cont. on next page.)

Joe was the most gifted of the four of us academically, finishing in the top 10 percent of his high school graduating class. Joe excelled musically as well and was involved with the choir and with school plays. His preparatory instrument into the realm of music was the flute. Within a few years after this initial introductory instrument, my parents invested in a Hammond organ. With private lessons, and preparations for competitions at the Illinois State Fair, Joe became quite a musician. He placed among the top two or three contestants every year he competed. Joe was the designated "entertainment" at East Aurora H.S. as the rest of us students filed into the auditorium before assemblies. There was even a time in college when he seriously considered a major in music.

Soccer and wrestling are two very important themes in the realm of sports for the Suhayda boys. Joe was involved heavily in both. He was a city of Aurora wrestling champion as a freshman in high school and would wrestle successfully on the varsity wrestling team at East Aurora. He played club soccer for the Aurora Kickers F.C. Soccer Club and played college soccer at the University of Illinois, and at Northern Illinois University as well. After college, Joe continued to play with the Kickers and became the clubs manager for a time. He also secured a referee's license and coached youth soccer for many years. During this time, Joe had the amazing opportunity to meet and have a beer with a countryman, and one of the most well known legends in soccer history, Ferenc Puskás.

Joe Married Rose Schlee,[22] in 1974 while she was working towards her Master's Degree. After receiving her Master's, Rose attended Loyola

---

back at least as far as my grandfather, who was also named Jozsef.

22 *Rose's family history is a very compelling one. Her parents literally walked out of Ukraine all the way to Germany to escape a famine caused by Joseph Stalin after the USSR took the country from its people. Stalin ordered a decree to the people of the country stating that the crops that they had been cultivating with their own hands no longer belonged to them. Further, he warned the people that if they tried to use those crops for their own purposes, he would have them executed. To further brutalize the people and bolster the wealth of the USSR, Stalin had 80 percent of the crops and grain produced in the Ukraine shipped to Russia. As a result, 7 million people in Ukraine died in a purposeful mass starvation of the country.*

and earned her Doctorate in 1990. Today, Rose is an Associate professor at Rush University Medical Center in the college of nursing. She is also an Associate Provost for program Evaluation for Rush University. They have two sons, Adam and Stephen. Joe and Rose raised their family in Woodridge, Illinois. Both Adam and Stephen finished college. Adam received his Bachelor's Degree from NIU in computer science and earned a Master's at DePaul University in computer programing. Steven received his Bachelor's Degree in Aviation Security from Lewis University after serving five years in the U.S. Marine corps.

Adam married his high school sweetheart Lauren Skeens. She is a nurse practitioner. Adam and Lauren are blessed with twin boys Eric and Andrew and live in Sugar Grove, Illinois.

Joe made his living in a sales and engineering career specializing in pump technology. Both Joe and Rose are enjoying their new roles as grandparents to Eric and Andrew.

"I have come a long way from the barefooted mischievous boy in a small village in Hungary, who enjoyed kicking a soccer ball, climbing trees, and playing tag with friends."

These are my brother's words to me in the email in which he furnished this history. Indeed he has come a long way across a vast ocean to another continent and across 60 years of time here in the U.S.

Lauren, Eric, Andrew, and Adam Suhayda

Back row L to R: Stephen, Rose, Joe Suhayda
Front row L to R: Flora Schlee, Laura Suhayda, Adam Suhayda

BIOGRAPHIES AND OTHER SHORT STORIES

László (Laci) (Leslie) Tamás Suhayda

Born: Pécs, Hungary
February 2, 1952

My mom purposefully didn't cut my younger brother's hair until he reached the ripe old age of three-and-a-half. Laci (Les) became the third male child born into our family in just five years. Sadly, my mom was zero for three in her desperate bid to give us a sister. My brother's long hair helped my mom hold on to the illusion of having given birth to a girl. I still remember when she finally relented and got Les his first haircut. My brother Joe and I just laughed and thought he looked ridiculous in his strange "boy" hair cut. Even at this point, for at least a short while, my mom had his hair cut only on the sides, leaving the top long and in a bun. My brother had beautiful, thick brown hair with chestnut highlights. I actually thought it a shame my mom cut his hair. Our neighbors looked at my brother with confusion at first, not knowing why my mom cut her cute little girl's hair so short. It was way past time to let the world know that my brother, Laci, was indeed my little brother and not my sister. Laci (Les) would not have long hair like this again until after he graduated high school in 1970. Long hair became fashionable for men by the mid 60s and on into the late 70s. It seems Les was ahead of his time.

As I've already mentioned, soccer and wrestling, were the two major sports in which the Suhayda boys excelled. Les was an outstanding wrestler at East Aurora High school, making the varsity team as a sophomore. He had already been the Aurora city champion in his weight class as a freshman, just as Joe and I had. An ankle injury, before the district meet in his senior year, destroyed his chances for a bid to continue in the state qualifying tournaments, which culminate in the state championships. Qualifying for the state wrestling tournament was a feat I knew he could have achieved had it not been for the unfortunate injury. Les already placed second in a very tough 16 team Palatine tournament, narrowly losing in the championship match. By most coaches judgements, this championship was a mini state tournament. Placing high in this competition worked as an accurate measurement of how these athletes might perform in the state series. This tournament featured some of the top high school wrestlers in the state of Illinois.

Disappointed but not beaten, Les continued a very successful athletic career after high school. The three of us played for the Aurora Kickers F.C. soccer club from the time we were young teens all the way through our adult years after college. The Kickers had been our springboard to our college soccer careers. Our initial contact with the game came in the form of street soccer before we left our native country. Playing for the Kickers was an extension of the European culture we came from. It was also a way in which we maintainied contact with people of Eastern European descent.

Les was being recruited by Lewis University's head soccer coach in the fall of 1970, but things didn't work out there. So after spending one year as a "Flyer," he came and joined me at Aurora College and became a Spartan. The college was eventually renamed Aurora University, after they developed a graduate program. We had the unique opportunity of playing together on the same college team. My brother Joe and I had a similar occasion at Northern Illinois University two years before. The TV show "Batman" was popular during this time. Les and I were quickly lampooned (in a good way) on campus by the nicknames of these two cartoon character super heroes. We were dubbed the "dynamic duo." We knew each other well on the pitch and collaborated effectively. After all, we played together all our lives. Les would make his "runs." It was my job to deliver the ball in a position where he could put it into the back of the net. I was the playmaker at midfield and Les became the dynamic striker and scorer of goals. In fact, Les set a scoring record that year which still stands at Aurora University. He had a remarkable eight assists and 22 goals in a 14-game schedule. Les's scoring, with a "few" assists from me, elevated our team to a conference championship. That was not the way things were supposed to happen, according to the pre-season forecasts. It is always great to prove the prognosticators wrong, especially when they bet against you.

War has a way of disrupting lives as my parents already knew. It was the Vietnam war that became a major disruptor of Les's education and soccer career at Aurora College. Vietnam was still raging in 1972, at the end of President Nixon's first term. So when Les learned he would be drafted into military service, he decided to take control of his now inevitable military service. He chose to enlist rather than allow himself to be drafted.[23] Les served 5 years in the U.S. Navy. The Navy was very good to him, even selecting Les to represent this branch of the military in the 1976 Olympic Soccer tryouts.

---

23 *Other sports accomplishments:* *All Conference and all NAIA District 20 pick in Soccer in 1971.* *Qualified for the NAIA National Wrestling Tournament at Aurora College in 1972.* *Coached for the NAS Meridian Base Team from 1973 to 1975.* *Coached the St. Louis Kickers U-14 team and won SLYSA and SCCYSA league championships.*

After my brother ended his active service with the Navy, he came back to play another year at Aurora College. He then moved south to St. Louis, and enrolled at Southern Illinois University in Edwardsville where he could be closer to Beth, his future bride. Les graduated from SIU in 1979 with a degree in Business Administration.

Les Married Elizabeth Ziegler on September 9, 1978. They have two children Laura and Matthew. They've been blessed with four grandchildren. Laura's three children are Nadia, Carson, and Kaden. Matt and Melissa Dutcher have one child, Eleanor. Beth retired as a middle school science teacher and was honored with the school district's Diamond Circle Award. She was also an Emerson Teacher of the year recipient and runner up in the Missouri State Teacher of the Year award.

Les is a self employed businessman and President of Laszlo Corporation. His company brokers chemical products to customers around the country. He is also a wine importer. Les is also the originator of the Menráthwine Slushee.

Les wrote this to me in the EMail in which he supplied this personal history.

"Freedom in the United States gives vision to those who can see opportunity. And that freedom paves the way to the ambition to achieve a better life."

L to R: Matthew, Elizabeth, Laura, and Les Suhayda

Eleanor Dutcher Suhayda
Daughter of Matt Suhayda and Melisa Dutcher

Back row L to R: Elizabeth Suhayda, Laura Suhayda
Middle row L to R: Helen Ziegler, Nadia Koper, Carson Koper
Front row L to R: Kaden Koper

BIOGRAPHIES AND OTHER SHORT STORIES

Marianna (Babi) Suhayda Rojas

Born: May 24, 1966
Aurora, Illinois

The fourth time was the charm for my mom. She finally got her little girl who is, for sure, the proverbial diamond in the rough among the Suhayda siblings. She is the rose among the thorns, although she has been known to have "sharp elbows" and occasionally a "sharp tongue." Marianna has either had the good fortune of having three brothers thirteen or more years older, or she has had the adversity of having been over parented by two biological parents and three much older siblings. I wouldn't want to venture a guess as to how she would answer that question. I've leaned to allow my sister to speak for herself. Suffice it to say she doesn't show any ill effects of having had three much older brothers. In fact, she has been known to put me in my place just a few times in recent history.

Our sister is a passionate person. She wears her heart on her sleeve, and it is a generous heart. Appropriately, her most important priority in life is her family. Her sons are her center. She is supportive of who they are, as well as what they do. That is also why she sets a high bar for them in all aspects of their lives. Babi balanced being a career person with being a full time mother. This came more out of necessity than choice. Robert, her husband, worked very successfully in the mortgage industry for many years until it's crash, starting in '05. When the housing market started to go "south," my sister went back to school full time to earn a nursing degree while working at Delnor Hospital in its Intensive Care Unit. She used this opportunity to learn on the job while at the same time applying that knowledge to the classroom setting. Babi graduated from Waubonsee Community College with a nursing degree (RN) in 2010. She went to work for DuPage Medical Group for a family practice office. She worked in this capacity for 3 years before accepting a position as a home health nurse. She was offered a position as a Nurse Case Manager. Then she was promoted to a position in which she assisted physicians and patients in developing treatment plans that enabled people to resume a semblance of their normal lives.

In her youth, our sister was accomplished musically and athletically as well. She played the hammond organ, the exact instrument our older brother Joe played. She picked up where Joe left off. She competed in the Illinois State Fair, as Joe had, and won the competition. She also competed in the Yamaha Contest and was runner up, twice. The soccer bug bit our sister as well. This is where those "sharp elbows" came into play. She played the sweeper back position, which is the heart of the defensive line. Babi was an accomplished gymnast as well. This training paid dividends in terms of helping her make the football and basketball cheerleading squads. Babi became the mascot (the Tomcat). This honor almost always goes to the most skilled gymnast on the team. She was one of just a few girls on the squad to be able to do back handsprings and back aerials.

Babi competed in the Miss United Teenager pageant in Bloomington-Normal, Illinois and was first runner up. She won Miss photogenic. Straight out of high school, Babi worked for Midway Airlines. She worked 5 years in downtown Chicago as a legal secretary. Her office had the most beautiful view of Lake Michigan. Her commute into the city got to be too complicated and time consuming. So she looked for employment closer to home in Aurora, and found it with Metropolitan Life Insurance Company. She worked for Metlife for 9 years and met Robert Rojas while there. They were married on June 16, 1995. They were blessed with two sons. Antonio, the eldest son, is currently attending Augustana College. He is in his freshman year. Marco, their second born, is a sophomore at Oswego High School.

When I asked Babi to furnish me with the details included in this bio, she put some of her heart into the project. Here is just one of the things she included that speaks to who she is as a person. "Success is not a measurement of what you possess. Success is a measurement of what you dare to achieve."

Back L to R: Marianna and Robert Rojas
Front L to R: Antonio and Marco Rojas

BIOGRAPHIES AND OTHER SHORT STORIES

Etta Suhajda Gönczi

Born: Dombegyház, Hungary
Oct. 5, 1939
Died: June 8, 2008

E tta, my cousin, came to us in Godisa about a year before my father's decision to leave Hungary. Her family at home was in disarray. Her father went to Budapest to work in the construction of the subway system. She didn't see much of him. She came to us in Godisa for salvation and also to find employment in Komló where both of my parents worked. My dad worked as a machinist making tools for excavation, while my mother worked to make the lamps used by the miners when they went below ground. Etta went to work for the water department for the city of Komlo. She was in charge of keeping track of water quality for the municipal water supply. She sampled the water for chlorine concentration.

I don't know for sure, but perhaps because of the family turmoil that she had been experiencing, she decided that she wasn't going back to her family in Dombegyház. Perhaps this was the reason she wanted to come with us. She made this fateful decision at age 16. My father didn't bat an eye in allowing her to come with us. This would later become a sore subject however, with Etta's Mom.

Etta was one of the nicest people I've ever had the pleasure of knowing. She never had a bad thing to say about anyone. She got along with everyone and always wore a smile. She met and then married Imre (Emri) Gönczi on Jan 2, 1960 at St. Nicholas church in Aurora, Ill. Emri had been a border guard on the Austrian border close to where we crossed into Austria before he decided to leave the country. Some of his fellow boarder guards simply decided to leave the country one day. Emri joined them fearing he may get into trouble if he came back alone. It is interesting to me that Emri defected almost in the same place that we had, and then came a half a world around to the same place we came as well.

Etta and Emri had three children Emri Jr., Clara Gönczi Coleman, and Steven Gönczi. Clara married Bruce Coleman. They have one adopted child Jennifer Coleman. Etta contracted a cancer and died June 8, 2008.

Etta Suhajda Gönczi

BIOGRAPHIES AND OTHER SHORT STORIES

Béla (Bill) Suhayda

Born: Pécs, Hungary
July 7, 1949

Graduation day was June 6, 1967. East Aurora High School would get increasingly smaller in the rear view mirror of my memory, but not for long. My brother Joe was already in college by this time and much of the money my parents earmarked for education of the Suhayda boys went with him to the University of Illinois. The wrestling coach at Western Illinois University was working to recruit me to wrestle for the Bulldogs. Jack Hughes "Big Jack" came to East with the coach to talk to me about wrestling for Western. Jack had been one of my idols when I was just a little junior high kid. He was a legendary football player and wrestler for East,[24] and he continued in that vein at Western. Now he was back, helping his coach in recruiting me to Western. I was flattered for the attention, however, my family didn't have the resources for me to enroll

---

24 *Jack would become a wrestling coach at West Aurora during the same time that I coached wrestling at East. We maintained a friendly rivalry.*

at the school. My mom and I made a college visit to Macomb, Illinois to further explore the possibilities. But it just wasn't going to be workable financially. Consequently, I attended Waubonsee Community College for the next two years.

After earning an Associate's Degree from Waubonsee in 1969, I took out a student loan and headed to Northern Illinois University (NIU) to play soccer for the Huskies. I joined many of my Kickers teammates, who were already playing there, including Axel Eder, George Jablonski, Eddie Kozitskiy, Henry Wind, Peter Glon, John Wells, Eric Roy,[25] and my brother Joe. Joe had transferred to NIU the year before. I would room with Al Zelachowski, our center back. Al had played for Maccabi, a rival of the Kickers. Foe became friend. We had a great team and a great season. In fact we had a national ranking in the top 20 teams in the country. Our only loss of the year came against the National Championship team of the previous year, the St. Louis Billikens. A very special person came into my life during this academic year. Her name was Brenda Shafer and she would become my bride. She also became my navigator and co-pilot while in the air, but more importantly, in my life. There were at least a few course corrections that became necessary.

Aurora College became my third stop on my way to a college degree. The costs of housing, tuition, and other living expenses at NIU were beyond what my meager finances could cover for a second year. I used up all of the money in the loan I took to attend Northern Illinois during my first year there. Working part time jobs and living at home to attend Aurora became plan "C." As I've already mentioned in my brother Les's bio, he and I collaborated in bringing a conference championship to Aurora in the Fall of 1971, when he joined me and the Spartans in that soccer season. We both had banner years, which made that season one of the most memorable athletic campaigns in all of my playing years.

25 *Eric's younger brother Willie Roy played for, and then coached the first professional soccer team in Chicago, The Sting. "The Sting, under Willie's tutelage, won an NASL Championship defeating the New York Cosmos 2-1 in 1981. The Cosmos had had some world class players playing for them including Pele, Franz Beckenbauer, and Johan Cruyff.*

Les enlisted into the Navy at the end of the 1971-72 school year, which left our team in need of scoring punch. Still, I had a good 1972-73 campaign, garnering All Conference, All District 20 honors along with being voted MVP by my teammates. I lead the team in assists and goals scored from a midfield position. I had one more year of eligibility at Aurora available to me, but decided I needed to grow up and stop playing games. These were almost my exact words to coach Bornkamp when he asked me to come see him in his office to plan the upcoming season. I decided that it was time I work to support myself and earn enough money to finish my education. In some ways I regret that decision now. Perhaps I should have taken out another loan.

Graduation from Aurora College came in the Spring of 1973 with a double major in Biology and Psychology and a minor in Chemistry. I thought my education was complete. But what I was going to do with my degrees, was an unanswered question at this point. A career in education was something that had been lurking in the back of my mind for a long time. But getting into teaching would require a teaching certificate. I had been working in the Department of Corrections at Valley View Boys School for a year as a youth supervisor/counselor. My decision was to go back to Aurora for one more year to get a teacher's certificate while continuing to work at Valley View. It was a hectic year, but at the end of it, I had the certificate and still managed to squeeze a private pilot's license into the mix.

My first teaching position was at The Faulkner School in Chicago as a science teacher. Faulkner was an all-Black private school with a population of about one hundred students. I was the science department. Accordingly, science department meetings were lonely and very short. There was, however, always plenty of seating. Questions were rare and there were only a few complaints. The commute to the south side of Chicago was an hour and a half from Westmont, Illinois where Brenda and I rented an apartment. The drive had become arduous and I had no desire to continue it for another year. I had no desire to live in the city either. After only one year at Faulkner, I resigned the position. Then, after a brief stint selling life insurance, my next teaching assignment took me back to my old public school district. I interviewed for a science position at K.D. Waldo Junior High and got lucky. In my second year, I also became the head wrestling coach at Waldo.

After five years and a transfer to East Aurora High School, coaching wrestling and teaching science brought me back full circle, to the teachers who mentored me, and to the wrestling program where I had been a competitor. I started the first soccer program at East Aurora in 1985, with a good amount of help from our new athletic director Cliff Pensyl, and a school district administrator Anna Sanford. Our district was the last to get a soccer program in our conference. In '91, I developed the Fox Valley Kickers Youth Soccer Club. And then in '99, I brought in the first girls soccer program to East. The Kickers youth club was affiliated with our old Aurora Kickers F.C. program, with which my brothers and I had played in our youth and through adulthood. We developed 14 teams before I resigned as president of the club. The Kickers youth club had become too time consuming for me, so I handed the program over to more capable hands, and went back to coach the varsity soccer team at East for the last 5 years of my education career. The club is still in existence today. It is exciting for me to drive around in Aurora and see the Kickers logos on the rear windows of vans carrying young soccer players.

It is also exciting for me to see my former players picking up the mantle of coaching, teaching, and living successful lives. Cam Leadbetter, a former student and wrestler came back to East to be a teacher, athletic director, and a dean of students. Frank Davison, who I coached in wrestling at Waldo, is now the head wrestling coach at East Aurora. Michael Glosson, a former soccer player of mine, now coaches basketball at Lake Park High School. Javier Hernandez, also a former Tomcat soccer player came back to East as a head coach for three seasons. Ricky DelTorro another soccer player of mine became the head coach at Marmion Academy. Gerardo Alvarez is an assistant coach at Benedictine University. Chris Hurst has become a successful business man, starting his own construction company. Tyler Johnson, a former soccer player, is now a police officer who very recently saved a woman's life when she submerged her van in a water retention pond. Rene Rodriguez, a very fine wrestler, has become an exemplary Christian man with love for his fellow man. Kenny Hartman a soccer player, and Roy Rodriguez, a former wrestler, became engineers, and Paulo Godinho coaches soccer at Lyons Township High School. Kurt Reuland and Kenny Hatcher have become very successful people in their own right. And there are many others, too many to mention here, who continue to make me proud to have had them as students and athletes.

After teaching the sciences/biology, and coaching for 25 years at East, I retired in 2005, having put in 30 years of service with School District 131, and three years with the Department of Corrections. Not totally ready for retirement, I worked as an assistant soccer coach at Aurora University for two years, and took the head soccer position at Newark High School for one year. A good friend and a former Aurora Police Officer, Lloyd Popp, called me to work for him at the Aurora Township, where I worked in a delinquency prevention program. Then, my former building principal at K.D. Waldo, Harrison Schneider, notified me of an opportunity to work with the Kane County Regional Office of Education in a truancy prevention program for District 131.

In 2012, I received one of the greatest athletic honors of my life. I was inducted into the Tomcat Athletic Hall of Fame for my wrestling accomplished as an athlete at East, and for the development of the soccer programs along with all my years of coaching wrestling, and soccer. My name, picture, and a short bio went up on the same walls as all of those amazing football players, wrestlers, and coaches I idolized as a junior high brat. It was a great honor!

My son Brett is now the Waubonsee Community College head soccer coach. Gibron Rodriguez and I are his assistants. We've worked together for seven years. Working with my son and Gibron has been one of the most rewarding experiences I've had in athletics. Brett took a program with one win in a season before he took the head position, to a team ranked seventh in the nation in 2013. The 2013 team also won both the Conference and Regional Championships. It was a historic year. No other team had achieved these milestones in school history. Brett was voted both soccer coach of the year, and over all coach of the year in the Skyway Conference. During the off season from coaching, Brett is playing for the Aurora Borealis. The Borealis is a semi professional soccer team in its first year of existence. C.J. Brown is our coach. C.J. played for the U.S. National team with a total of 15 international appearances. He was also a player for the Chicago Fire, and then became an assistant coach for the Fire after retiring as a player. I am working with the owner of the Borealis, Tim Cottingim, along with C.J., in a consulting capacity as we develop the team.

Brett became my "tag along" in his early youth when I was coaching high school wrestling and soccer. He was on our bus rides to many contests. So these two sports became ingrained and a part of his everyday experience. Having me as his father gave him no chance to escape that influence. Needless to say, he took to both sports like a duck to water. Brett became a member of the first soccer team I put together for the Fox Valley Kickers Youth Soccer Club. Gibron Rodriguez, was also a member of that team. Brett started wrestling at age four for the Tomcat Wrestling Club. He was an amazing little wrestler with win records over ninety percent almost every year. He continued to wrestle all the way through college at Lawrence University.

Brett graduated from Lawrence in 2005 with a biology degree. While at Lawrence, he played soccer for the Vikings. With the exception of five minutes in a Beloit game, he had an amazing record of having played every minute of every game for four years. He was selected to the all conference teams in his junior and senior years. He was also an all Wisconsin select player in his junior year. He was a captain for the Vikings in his junior and senior years as well. Brett was inducted into the Oswego High School Athletic Hall of fame in 2011. After obtaining his bachelor's degree, he entered into a Master's program at the University of Massachusetts. After finishing a masters degree in plant and soil science, he went to work for ENCAP. He continues to work for ENCAP, in the position of project manager and estimator. The company specializes in ecological restoration. Brett also has a solo pilot's license. He is the third generation of aviators in the family. I'm hoping that string continues.

My daughter Stephanie has blessed our family with two wonderful babies. They are Alyssa and Audrey. Brenda and I have them one day of the week. They are keeping us young. Stephanie became a beautiful dancer, having started dance at the tender age of 4. She was pulling herself up on furniture and bouncing to music even before she took her first steps. Seeing her enthusiasm for music, we enrolled Stephanie into a park district program first, and then into Bonnie Ardelean Dance Studio at age 6. She and a good friend, Holly Johnson, performed "Marian the Librarian" in a play at the Paramount Theater in Aurora called "The Music Man." They were 10 at the time. Stephanie advanced to the ultimate in ballet technique...pointe ballet. As a 15-year-old, she and a friend, Laura Burke, qualified for a national competition held in Orlando, Florida. They performed "Drigo Divertissements." Stephanie would eventually dance every style of dance taught at Bonnie's. Her favorite remained ballet. She performed at North Central College in a Dance West Studio presentation of "The Nutcracker Suite." She appeared in "Marzipan," "Spanish," (chocolate), "Snow," and "Waltz of the Flowers." Steph created magic when she danced. She danced so beautifully that both Brenda and I would tear up watching her. Stephanie graduated from North Central College in 2003 with a business degree. She currently works for "Snoopy" at Metropolitan Life Insurance Company in Aurora as a Client Service Consultant. It is a great irony that Stephanie took part in dance performances at MetLife as a young girl when Brenda worked there.

I met Brenda while attending Northern Illinois University in DeKalb, Illinois. A couple of friends, Sharla Nimerfroh and Vicki Moran stopped to pick Brenda up one evening saying that they needed more girls to meet some of the players on the NIU soccer team. Brenda didn't meet me on this occasion, however. She met my brother Joe. Then, weeks later at the Student Union, George Jablonski, a teammate, and I were attending a dance when we bumped into Brenda and Sharla. They were leaving the dance as we were arriving. We stopped to chat, and then Sharla invited all of us to a "get together" at her parents house. Sharla was already playing cupid in getting Brenda and I together.

When Brenda learned I was a Hungarian immigrant, her imagination got the best of her. For some reason, she had the notion I might be a Hungarian prince. Unfortunately for her, she found out I was a Hungarian pauper instead. But she forgave me, and we did start seeing each other on a regular basis. At first glance, I was afraid she might still be in high school. Then I learned that she had just graduated from Sycamore High School, and was already working for an insurance agency. That made her seem accountable, and a mature young lady. I was impressed she was already fully employed, and appeared responsible. The fact she was very pretty became an added bonus. We continued to date even after I left DeKalb to attend Aurora College.

Brenda moved out of her parents home, to St. Charles, Ill., after getting a new job with American States Insurance company in Carol Stream, Illinois. She roomed with my brother Joe's girlfriend, soon to be wife Rose Schlee. She lived much closer to me now, and our relationship became more serious. Eventually, Brenda and I moved into an apartment in Batavia. Then, when my first teaching position took me to Chicago, we moved to Westmont, Illinois to be closer to work. Brenda now worked for a quirky, but likable Jake P. Sommers at Oakbrook Insurance Agency. Jake was a great guy and very funny. He was one of those people you had to love, even if you didn't quite understand why. He was very loyal to Brenda, and stuck up for her when customers became insulting. He would rather tell a customer to take their business elsewhere than have Brenda put up with disrespect or uncivil treatment. Jake survived things in the business world most others would not have. Brenda's next job took her to Plapp Insurance Agency in Berwyn, Illinois.

Brenda and I were married on July,16, 1977 in a ceremony conducted by her uncle, Rev. Gordon Shafer, at the United Methodist Church in Sycamore, Illinois. Our honeymoon took us to Hungary where we visited with my father's relatives in Budapest. From there we went to Hoszuhetény (hoe-sue-hetane), a suburb of Pécs, where my mom's family was located. This had only been my second visit back to Hungary since our escape in 1956. All defectors who left at the time of the revolt, had been given amnesty by this communist regime by this time. To a great degree, this was by necessity. It seems that the communists needed capitalist dollars, (tourism), in order to keep themselves solvent. The economy of the country was very poor as evidenced by dilapidated infrastructure and homes. They needed Western currencies that had value, and at this point, it didn't even matter to them that much of this money coming into the country was coming from former defectors they would have killed at the border just 20 years before.

Both Brenda and I were just a little concerned getting onto a train leaving Vienna bound for Budapest. The train we just left, coming from Frankfurt, was clean, opulent and roomy. This Hungarian train we were boarding was dirty, dilapidated, cramped, and had armed soldiers carrying rifles on their shoulders. The comparison of these two trains reflected perfectly the difference between people who live under tyranny and those who live in freedom. The conditions that existed on this train were certainly an interesting way for this communist regime to throw out the "RED" carpet for us and other tourists. I was embarrassed by the poor first impression Brenda must have had of Hungarian culture. After our return to the states, my relatives wrote to tell my parents that Brenda and I had been followed by secret service personnel everywhere we went in the country. My father's antics in 1974 may have had something to do with the scrutiny we were being given.[26]

---

26 *During a visit back to Hungary and his hometown Kisdombegyház in 1974, my father*
(cont. on next page.)

Brenda started work on a bachelor's degree in 1975. She took one or two courses at a time at the College of Dupage. Then when I was hired at Waldo, we moved to Aurora, and she continued taking classes at Waubonsee Community College. She became a full time student at NIU in 1979. She graduated from Northern in 1981 with a bachelor's degree in education. She received her diploma on a warm spring day and five months pregnant with our daughter, Stephanie. We used to kid my daughter at having graduated college twice in her lifetime.

After getting her degree in education, Brenda substitute taught until Brett was born. In the fall of 1983, she worked as a Chapter 1 teacher (reading teacher) and Gifted Program teacher in School District 131. Brenda secured a teaching position at West Aurora School District 129 teaching a fifth/sixth grade combination elementary class.

Brenda left education after having been a teacher for close to six years. She went to work at MetLife for eight years before going to United Chambers Insurance company. The company was in trouble financially so Brenda went to HEREIU (International Welfare Fund) later to become UNITE HERE HEALTH. She was a senior with the company and began working with a programmer who had developed a computer program for paying claims. Up to this point, health claims were processed by human hands. She then was put into a position where she also did programming to further develop this system of automated claim payments. She did this with little to no training. It was a job she learned simply by doing. Brenda worked for the company for 15 years, retiring in September of 2013.

One of the greatest pleasures Brenda and I enjoyed in our lives has been to watch our children grow into the competent, strong people they are today. We have a tremendous amount of pride in our children. I often tell Brenda how lucky we have been to have two such talented, wonderful children. We are also pleased with the choices our children made in terms

---

hosted a get together for the village at a local restaurant. My father placed American flags on all of the tables in the establishment while the food was being served. Subsequently, he was banned from ever returning to the country. (see bio for Suhayda Lajos Zoltán)

of who they chose for their spouses. Brian Evans, my daughter's husband, is a devoted father to his two darling little girls Alyssa and Audrey. He is also a caring, supportive person to our daughter Stephanie. Brian works for Carol Stream Public Works Department as a utility supervisor. Stephanie and Brian were married on Sept. 10, 2010. Joanna Schander Suhayda is a beautiful, understanding, and thoughtful young woman. She works as a billing and accounts manager for Midwestern Contractors. Brett and Joanna met in Appleton, Wisconsin while attending Lawrence University. They were married on Oct. 1, 2011. We couldn't have picked better people than Brian and Joanna as spouses for our children, even if we tried.

Brenda and Bill Suhayda wedding photo.

Joanna Schander Suhayda and Brett M. Suhayda

Brenda and Bill Suhayda, 2016

Stephanie Suhayda Evans and Brian Evans

Audrey and Alyssa Evans, daughters of Stephanie and Brian Evans

AFTERWORD

A WORD OR TWO ABOUT SOME VERY SPECIAL

TEACHERS AND MENTORS OF MINE

JOHN HENRY HINCK: I met John in the summer of 1961. I was about to make the big move from Brady Elementary School to the lofty academic world of C.F. Simmons Junior High School. John was repairing a sidewalk at Brady as I casually walked by. He asked me where I would be going to school during the next school year. When I told him I would be attending Simmons, he told me it was very likely I would be a student of his during the next school year. When I asked him why, he simply told me he was going to be teaching at Simmons. To this point, I only associated the spreading of chalk on blackboards in terms of what teachers did with their hands. I hadn't seen teachers laboring physically before. Spreading cement with a trowel seemed out of character in terms of what an educator might do. And of course they never left their school buildings. The classroom walls absorbed them when the day was done. They would magically reappear the next day before we arrived. But in reality, teachers in these days worked all kinds of odd jobs to make ends meet. Working maintenance for their school districts was one of the best jobs male teachers could get during summer breaks. John didn't take summers off..

I don't know who among our classmates"christened" John as "Clark Kent," but it was a great stroke of genius. I understood perfectly why the name was so appropriate. John possessed the stature and good looks of George Reeves, the actor who played the famous superhero, Superman, in the weekly T.V. series by the same name. John even had the same "crew cut" as Clark. John also wore the same dark rimmed glasses, which worked as the perfect disguise that concealed Superman's identity and converted him into the hapless newspaper reporter Clark Kent. All John would have needed in his classroom was a telephone booth and we would have all been convinced of who he really was. To me, he was and remains a super guy.

John was a special person for me in my Jr. High years. The reasons I liked him so much had to do with his huge outgoing personality, and because I always got the sense that he cared a great deal about his students and athletes. He set a high bar of expectation for us. When he did that, we got the sense he had confidence in our abilities to achieve. John's attention for us was genuine. It was genuine and it was bigger than life because he stood 6'4 in his flat heeled black or brown wing tips. I felt distinctly honored when I became a student in his science class in my eighth grade year. Kids bragged about who their teachers were when they thought them to be cool. Everyone bragged about having Mr. Hinck as their teacher, including me.

John had and still has a personal touch with everyone he meets. I tried to emulate this style of working with students and parents when I became an educator and coach myself. What I discovered was that the benefits of caring about people came back to the giver many fold. I owe this revelation to his example. As one of his students, I felt I could rise above obstacles simply because of his example of optimism.

John had a meteoric rise through the ranks of school administration in School District 131, becoming Superintendent of Schools just twelve years after I saw him repairing that sidewalk at Brady School. He went from grade school teacher at Hermes Elementary School, to a science teacher at Simmons, and then transferred to East Aurora High School as a P.E./ science teacher. I believe he did all of this by design. Seeing education at all of these different developmental levels gave him an understanding of the educational system top to bottom. I'm convinced that the reasons for his quick rise administratively were not only because of his competence and professionalism as an educator, but also because of the caring and kind person John was and still is.

GORDON POSTLEWAITE: Gordie was another Simmons Junior High teacher for whom I had admiration. But for Gordie, I had a certain amount of "fearful" respect as well. He was the science teacher right next door to John Hinck. That made traversing the west hallway at Simmons a gauntlet for neck squeezing by Mr. Hinck and loud interrogations by Gordie. John and Gordie would stand in the west hallway, during passing period, grabbing and engaging their athletes and students as they walked by. Some of us would even go out of our way to walk down that hallway just so we could be in the presence of their good humor and energy. Gordie had a booming voice. He had a raucous laugh and a quick smile that could turn into an instant frown if he saw or heard something displeasing. I think it was this quick change in mood that put just a little bit of fear in me as a junior high student. It sometimes came unexpected. I would learn later he did this for effect more than anything else. But I got the sense you never wanted to "cross" Gordie. You had to watch your "P's" and "Q's" with him. "Don't get on his wrong side" was the word on Gordie. He had a huge personality that took up the entire room or hallway he happened to be in. Everyone else took a back seat except maybe John Hinck.

I wouldn't have ever guessed in these formative years that Gordie would play a very important, and even pivotal role in my career as an educator. My brother Joe attended a class reunion after high school. Gordie was in attendance and in a conversation they had, Gordie would find out that I finished my first year of teaching at The Faulkner School on the southside of Chicago. Because of a difficult and time-consuming commute into Chicago, I was not returning to teach there. I was out of a job and perhaps even out of education after I resigned my position with the school. I just started a sales career, selling life insurance with Fidelity Union Life Insurance. Gordie informed Joe of two science positions open in his school district, School District 131, if I was interested in applying. One of these positions was in his building at Simmons, where Gordie was now Principal. The other position was at K.D. Waldo Junior High School. Joe called me to tell me of the good news and I called Gordie to set up an interview for the position at Simmons. We had the interview and Gordie offered me the position. But I had some good success in the sales world and asked Gordie if I could have some time to think it over. I dithered, so by the time I called Gordie back, the position at Simmons had been filled. Not missing a beat, Gordie said I should apply for the other position at Waldo. I applied and got it. I didn't hesitate to take this job when it was offered. I learned a valuable lesson about grabbing opportunities when they were presented. And so I would spend the next 30 years as an educator in School District 131, the same district in which I had been a student. I have Gordie to thank for this good fortune. Years later I would have Gordie as my building principal at East Aurora High School ...my alma mater. He was, by far, the best principal I would have at East High. A very interesting detail about Gordie is that he was a regent at Carthage college in Kenosha, Wisconsin. Incredibly, he has this honor in common with our 16th president of the United States, Abraham Lincoln. I would find this out on a trip I made to Carthage with my son, Brett, when he was considering attending the school.

DICK PAUL: We called Mr. Paul "Popeye." If you've ever seen this cartoon character, you know he has the odd physical characteristic of having inordinately large forearms. Dick's right forearm has the appearance of being much larger than his left. The reason for this abnormality has to do with an injury he sustained to his right elbow. The injury prevented him from totally straightening his elbow. It also creates the illusion his right forearm is bigger than his left.

Dick was a sixth grade teacher at Brady while I was in attendance there. All of the sixth graders wanted to be in his class. I was one of the unfortunates to not have the good luck to be one of his students, however. All the boys wanted to be in his class because we thought he was "cool" and because he was a young male teacher. All of the girls wanted to be in his class because they had crushes on him. Dick became a math teacher at Simmons junior high when I became a student there. Dick then transferred to East High as a math teacher. He was also a track coach at Simmons and then at East High after his transfer. We became colleagues, (partners in crime) after I started teaching at East more than twenty years later. He had those same qualities as Gordie and John in inspiring you to be better than you thought you could be. It was a kind of motivation the teachers of that time could manifest. Unfortunately, I no longer see the strong personalities in education I enjoyed as a student. These men inspired us solely because of their presence. It was the force of their personalities that motivated us. We didn't want to disappoint Dick, John or Gordie on the athletic field or in the classroom. We ran faster, and studied harder because we wanted to please Mr. Paul. But he was not just an amazing and demanding coach, he was also an educator. I got the sense that he was an educator first. He came from a time when the term "student athlete" was taken seriously.

DEL DUFRAIN: Del was our football coach at East Aurora High School, and that alone made him a god in my eyes. He was an iconic figure for me especially in my junior high years. During football seasons, the teachers at Simmons would talk of the great teams that played and were playing at East Aurora. I was almost in disbelief I would eventually have the honor of attending this magical high school that all these brave athletes attended. I would be sitting in the same desks and walking the same hallways as these gladiators. I attended most of the games and watched the "wars" that took place under the lights and in front of thousands of enthusiastic fans on Roy E. Davis field. Del, always dressed in a suit, tie, overcoat and a trilby hat on the sideline of these games. He was the face of East Aurora Football. He was the orchestrator of all the glorious Tomcat teams. These games were community events broadcast on radio and covered by the Aurora Beacon Newspaper. It was all bigger than life drama for me.

Del became one of my biology teachers during my sophomore year. The class was team taught by Gordie Postlewaite, Lee Whitt, and Del. Mr. Witt would set up the labs on Tuesdays and Thursdays. Del and Gordie did the lectures on the alternate days. Then as a senior, I had advanced biology with Del. It was about this time, during my senior year, that I started to strongly consider going into the sciences in college. It was mostly due to this man that I had made that decision. By this time, I came to the realization that Del was not only a great coach, but he was also a great educator. Del was gracious and professional in his approach to his craft. I never saw him flustered by anything or anyone. He had a calm optimistic exterior. Whether in a tight football game, or in a "situation" with an unruly student, he was composed, collected, and a class act. In the classroom, he made only rare references to football or even athletics. It simply wasn't the place or time for such discussions. When in a biology classroom, he taught biology. And the breadth and depth of his understanding of his subject matter was impressive. He delighted in the subject matter. The love he had for teaching and for nature was obvious. One of the greatest honors Del would ever pay me was coming to the Upstate Eight conference wrestling tournament, in my senior year, where I wrestled for a conference championship. After I came off the mat, he came over to personally congratulate me with a firm handshake. It was one of those moments in my young life in which I felt that I had "arrived."

Then in the year I was working to earn a teacher's certificate at Aurora College, I would have the honor to return to East and have Del as a supervisor in what was termed a "Pre-teaching" experience. This was a precursor to my student teaching. Nine years later, after getting a transfer from Waldo Junior High to East High to teach Biology and coach wrestling, I would teach in Lee Whitt's former classroom next to Del's. I had gone from admiring this master coach and teacher as a junior high kid, to working with him in the science department at my alma mater. Del and I worked collaboratively as biology teachers in adjoining rooms. I continued to learn from him even at this juncture of my life. Just this year, he sent me one of his pride and joy possessions. It was the microscope he used when demonstrating microscope technique for his students. Grayal Gilkey, an English teacher and a former East Aurora basketball coach...one of the smartest and wittiest men you would ever want to know, brought the microscope back with him from a visit he had with Del in Wisconsin. It is the same scope he used when I sat in his class as one of his students my sophomore year.

BOB HURD: Bob was a "hard ass" with a southern drawl and great heart. He was my P.E. teacher and the man who was instrumental in getting me into wrestling. Having been a drill sergeant in the military, he ran his P.E. classes as if he was training soldiers for combat. Just as in the military, he used peer pressure to keep us in line. If we had "bad actors" in our midst, just as in the military, he punished the entire group for the sins of the few. One of his favorite punishments was to have us extend our arms out in front of us and then hold them there until he allowed us to put them down. At first, we would think this was easy and even silly. But the smirks on the faces soon turned to expressions of pain the longer he kept us in this position. Then he let us put our arms down. As soon as we had another immature outburst, we would be back in a straight line with our arms extended again. He would walk up and down the line, twirling his whistle and staring us down talking about the importance of a disciplined body and mind.

I would later learn this was also one of the ways he would pick the members of his wrestling teams. Those boys who quit early, and those who easily gave up the fight to keep their arms up were disqualified from consideration for his program. Mr. Hurd took notice of those of us who showed pride, determination and a stubborn attitude not to be beaten by pain. My obstinate resolve to not allow myself to be beaten by this "exercise" or by anyone else in the class in fighting fatigue and pain caught Mr. Hurd's attention. So when winter came and it was wrestling season in my seventh grade year, Mr. Hurd came to me and gave me an invitation to join the wrestling team he started at Simmons. I didn't much like him at this stage of our relationship, but I saw a completely different side to this man once he became my coach. I was also very surprised and even flattered that this tough man considered me worthy enough to be on his team. He was a Dr. Jekyll and Mr. Hyde kind of personality. I liked Dr. Jekyll much better than the Mr. Hyde alter ego I came to know in gym class. Bob Hurd made me tougher than I ever thought I could be in his wrestling room. I was the smallest kid in the room at about 4'9", and weighing only 75 pounds, so my sparring partners were always bigger, and usually stronger. But he would encourage me to take on these bigger, stronger opponents. He talked about how much tougher I would be if I wrestled these kids. He explained I would have to be more determined, smarter, quicker, and have better skills in order to have wins on these practice mats.

In gym class, when we had our wrestling units, he would put me out front and center and pick kids much bigger and stronger than I was, and have me wrestle them. He prefaced the matches by saying things like "It's not the size of the dog in the fight, it is the size of the fight in the dog, that determines who wins." Then he would blow the whistle to start the matches and I would have to go about proving he was right. The pressure was huge, but I can honestly say I never made a liar out of Mr. Hurd in this regard.

I think back on Mr. Hurd with great fondness. He taught me how to be tough. He also taught me how to be smart in an uneven physical contest. He taught survival, as all good warriors do.

ROY FOWLEY: Roy became my high school wrestling coach at East Aurora High School. Roy had a wide repertoire of physical abilities, and he was great at all of them. In the wrestling room, he was a technician. He taught technique through repetition. So to learn from Roy, you had to fight boredom just a little because of his attention to minor adjustments in technique. But as they say, "the devil is in the detail." What I learned from Roy gave me an upper hand with most of my opponents.

JAMES VALESANO: James Valesano was our principal at Simmons Junior High. He commanded respect just with his presence. He stood in front of his microphone before assemblies, staring at us. When we finally succeeded in shushing our fellow classmates into some semblance of order, he stood there for another 10 seconds or so. Then when you could almost hear a pin drop, he admonished us for our rudeness. However, he did this by appealing to our pride. He would say, "I know you can do much better than this." Then he would look at us some more for effect. By the end of every school year, we would become orderly on these occasions almost immediately. He understood operant conditioning well. I would have Mr. Valesano as a professor at Aurora College when I went back for a certificate to teach. He said something in one of those classes that stuck with me throughout my career as an educator. We were discussing how teachers needed to be leaders in the classroom and in our schools and communities. He said something that, at first, I thought to be a little odd for a former administrator and principal. He said that if a teacher goes through an entire career without having been written up for disciplinary reasons, that person didn't qualify as a teacher . He suggested that such a person didn't exhibit the passion necessary to do the job of educating. Mr. Valesano valued independent strong personalities in his faculty.

DON GOVONI: Don became my other wrestling coach at East. He was by far the tougher of my two wrestling coaches. Where Roy used subtle technique, Don used brute force. Where Roy wanted us to use force, Don would use even greater force. He told us the story about his high school state championship match in which he literally knocked out his opponent. None of us doubted his word. We didn't dare. Don demonstrated what he called "the half inch punch" on me. He said it was a "technique" used to distract an opponent in order to hit a double leg takedown. But the way Don used this "distraction," there would be little need to actually hit the move. The opponent would most likely go to the mat by shear gravity alone. After all, it is difficult to stay on your feet in a state of unconsciousness. My teammates would ask Don for repeats on this particular technique. For some strange reason, they were intrigued at watching my hair fly around and my head jerk backward during this demonstration. The technique seemed obvious enough to me after a half-dozen demonstrations. Yet my team mates clamoured for more examples. I didn't believe my teammates needed all this clarification. But Don was more than willing to repeat the trauma to my mandible in order to get his point across. I always came away from these sessions with a jaw that was just a little painful to close.

East Aurora "Upstate Eight Conference Championship team '67

Back Row L. to R. Coach Roy Foley, Frank Ortiz, Chris Swanson,
Steve Kenyon, Chuck Robinson, Dennis Stenson, Cecil McClain,
Team Mgr., Coach Don Govoni

Front Row L. to R. Roy Shermerhorn, Marchus Bachmeier, Warren Bauman,
Chris Quigley, Bill Suhayda, Vince Testone, Dave Hett

JOHN STRUCK: John was my supervising teacher during my student teaching days at C.F. Simmons Junior High. John has a great wit and an easy manner. He has an uncanny ability to make people feel comfortable with a light joke. He also has a sharp intellect that will surprises you. He can operate freely and easily between moments of humor and more serious issues. John has some of the same great qualities of John Hinck. It is not by accident that they are good friends. John also had a very quick rise through the ranks of administrators in school district 131, ultimately becoming Assistant Superintendent. And for a good while, all teachers in 131 understood John to be in charge, not the person in the Superintendent's office.

HARRISON SCHNEIDER: Harrison was my building principal at Waldo Junior High. He is one of those rare intellectuals I've known who has a basic ability to perceive, understand, and judge things in ways that are shared by most other people. Harrison is a historian by education. He is also a problem solver and one of the most sane people I have ever known. He has a knack of looking at problems and coming up with quick, easy common sense solutions. He is an unflappable guy with an easy smile and graceful humility. Harrison was one of only a few administrators I had the pleasure of knowing during my educational career, who was also universally liked by his faculty. He is from Long Island, a name he loves to mispronounce as "Lon-Giland."

THE AURORA KICKERS F.C. SOCCER CLUB was founded in 1959, the year after we came to town in Aurora, Illinois. Some of the founders of the Kickers were George Zielbauer, Joe Zielbauer, Simon Klambauer, Hermann Friedmann, Joe Mehlmann, and Ehrhardt Stallman. The first manager of the club was a "kind of" Kirk Douglas look alike, Philipp Reis. If it hadn't been for these men, the Suhayda boys would never have had the great pleasure or opportunity for playing their native game of "Futball." Ironically, the Zielbauer brothers and Simon Klambauer, had been born and lived in Hungary. Simon actually lived just 30 miles from where I was born. Joe Mehlmann was just across the border in Croatia, not more than an hour from the small village in which I grew up. They, like my mom's family, were of German heritage, and found themselves spread out in other Eastern European countries. Maria Theresa, an Austrian queen, repopulated Hungary and other Eastern European countries with Austrians and Germans after the Turks wiped out a large percentage of these countries' populations in the Ottoman Wars between the thirteenth and eighteenth centuries. I found it ironic we traveled halfway around the world to join up with people who came from the same part of Europe. They were from a place just a few hundred kilometers apart from where we originated.

Back Row: Joe Vizgirda, Ehrhardt Stallman, Peter Glon, George Zielbauer, John Fisher, Joe Suhayda, Hermann Friedmann, Joe Mehlmann, Bill Suhayda, Phillip Ries Front Row: Unknown, Joe Zielbauer, Peter Gross, Ray Roy, Eric Roy, Eddie Guerra, Axel Eder, Arnold Schili

Back Row: Phillip Riess, Eric Roy, Unknown, Cornell Kreiger, Herman Kreiger, Joe Zielbauer, Carl Baesler, Erhart Stallman, Kickers Queen, Joe Vizgirda, George Zielbauer Front Row: Arnold Shili, Joe Mehlmann, Henry Wind, Hermann Friedman, Les Suhayda, Bill Suhayda

These men donated their time and efforts to work with my brothers and I in developing us not only as soccer players, but also as human beings, and ultimately as friends. They provided the coaching, the transportation, and the moral support that developed us into the players we became. Other contemporaries of ours with the Kickers were Arnold Schili, Axel Eder, Eric Roy, Klaus Weber, George Jablonski, and Eddie Guerra. My brothers and I owe a debt of gratitude to the Aurora Kickers organization for the friendships and opportunities they provided for us in the game of "Futball."

VITO and JANE CARELLO: Vito was one of our childhood friends, right off the boat, after we arrived in Ishpeming, from the refugee camp in New Jersey. Unfortunately, we lost contact with him and the rest of our friends and acquaintances on the U.P. after we left in 1958. Then in 1993, 35 years later, I took my wife, Brenda, and my children on a visit to Ishpeming. It was still the same little town I remembered. It showed little signs of having changed, other than it looked more impoverished now. It had been a mining town since its inception. Much of the mining shut down by now, going back to the late 1960s. I looked for the two homes we lived in and succeeded in finding the second, on Barnum Street. This was the home in which we lived just before we left for Aurora. The Carnegie Library and the Mather Inn worked as great landmarks in the find. Emboldened by the discovery, I went on the more challenging hunt of finding the first house we were placed into on a temporary basis. This house was relocated in order to make room for the construction of a middle school. This is also the reason we were moved out of the home. I had no idea where it had been reestablished. I saw an elderly lady tending a garden in the vicinity of the middle school. I thought maybe a person her age, if she lived in this neighborhood at the time of the construction of the school, would know where the house had been relocated. To my amazement, she knew exactly where the house had been moved. I went to the address, recognized the house, and knocked on the door. There was no answer. I spent a few minutes looking at the structure, reminiscing about those days of my youth when we lived in this home. Then as I was driving away, I saw a pickup truck driving in the direction of the house. I followed the movement of the truck in my rear view mirror and saw it pulling into the driveway of our old house. I went back and knocked on the door for a second time. A man I considered to be close to my age answered the door. I explained to him what I was doing and asked if I could come in and walk through the house "for old times sake." To my astonishment, the man knew who I was. He remembered the Hungarian family that lived in the house for just a short time. He had actually been a neighbor of ours when we lived in this home. He introduced himself as Vito, and even asked if I might be Joe, my older brother. Vito now owned the home. We had a couple of beers and I caught Vito up on what happened to us since we left town. We exchanged eMail addresses and for a while kept track of each other electronically. But life gets busy with children and work, and the eMail he gave me was no longer working. Once again, we lost contact.

In the summer of 2015, I went back to Ishpeming for only the second time since we had left the community in the summer of 1958. Once again I was on the hunt for that first house and Vito if he still lived in the house. But it had been twenty two years since I'd been in Ishpeming and things were not looking familiar. Brenda (my wife) and I went to city hall and asked if they had any records of where homes may have been relocated when the middle school was built. We didn't get solid information about where we could locate the home, but we got a kind of ball park guess from the people in the office. I had good faith I would recognize the area once I was in the neighborhood. As we drove in the vicinity of where we were told the house may be located, we drove by a beautiful yellow victorian home with a wrap around porch. As we went by, we saw a man and a woman, presumably husband and wife, enjoying a tea and a beer on the porch. We must have looked a little suspicious driving so slowly, scrutinizing the area the way we were. The couple on the porch looked at us as we looked back at them. Then Brenda suggested we go back and ask these people if they knew anything about the house that we were looking for. I thought it was a great idea. After all, I wanted to get a better look at this beautiful old home that had tweaked my interest as we had driven by the first time.

I parked the car and went back. They were still there enjoying the warm summer weather and a cool drink. When I told the couple what I was doing, the guy invited Brenda and I to join them on the porch. As I am walking up onto the porch, he says to me, "You're Béla, aren't you!" It was Vito.

STEVE (BENNY) KENYON: It is much easier to see integrity in our mentors than in our friends and colleagues. Benny is a friend and a colleague who is an exception to this rule. I had the great pleasure to work with and learn from Benny over many years of coaching and teaching at East Aurora. Benny and I were on the same East Aurora wrestling team in the late 1960s. We were now teaming up again, as coaches at our alma mater. It was because Benny needed an assistant wrestling coach that I transferred to East High. In the time he and I worked together, I also learned he is one of the best competitors I have ever known. I don't mean that he was a prolific winner of contests. Nor did his wrestlers or the football teams he coached have huge numbers of championships. Mind you, Benny had a good degree of success in terms of wins and losses, as an athlete and as a coach. But he was successful in other, more important ways.

There is a type of competitor who believes there is much more to winning than just winning. He believes life can be taught through athletics. He believes the process in the preparation for victory is more important than the result. He also believes how an athlete wins is as important as the victory itself. This kind of athlete believes fair and honest competition should be a universal aim all athletes and coaches strive to achieve. After all, winning any other way makes for hollow meaningless victories. Winning by either cheating or great fortune does not reveal much about the competitor, except that they are either dishonest or lucky. It doesn't measure any of the things essential to being a good or competent athlete or person. For this reason, winning as a result of skill, athleticism, preparation and determination should be the aim of any competitor. We can only be assured of our competence as athletes if we win by our strategies, skills, and sweat. These measures tell us who we are in the arena. These are the things that give us pride in who we are, not only as athletes, but also as honorable human beings. This is a lesson I learned from Benny. And I didn't learn this from him by his word. I learned it by deed.

Benny lives this idea of competition because he is a man who accepts life as it comes to him. He lives an honest life. He lives by his word and he doesn't need to change the truth. If you ever want to be entertained by the folly of life in athletics, park yourself in a chair next to him and listen to the amazingly amusing and compelling stories he has to offer.

KLAUS WEBER: My granddaughter Alyssa talks about first best friends all the time. I'd like to say a few words about Klaus, my first best friend here in the states. We met as he sidled up next to me at a couple of urinals in my first day at Brady Elementary. He found out I was a recent immigrant, probably from Mrs. Robert, our fourth grade teacher. So he took the occasion, during recess, to have a conversation with me as we urinated in unison. He informed me he was from Germany and that he needed a soccer partner with whom he could continue to hone his skills.[27] I was more than willing to oblige. We have had long periods when we have not seen each other through the years. Whenever we do meet, we pick up exactly where we left off. First best friends! I think there must be something special about urinal bonding time.

L to R: Joe, Bill, and Les Suhayda

27 *Soccer, here in the states, was almost an unknown sport at this time.*

MORE HISTORICAL PHOTOS

Brenda

Brenda and I at Lake Geneva Wisconsin with our beautiful granddaughters Alyssa and Audrey Evans.

The infamous Me-109 (Messerschmidtt Bf-109) My father flew this plane in WWll against the Russians on the Eastern Front.

The acorn doesn't fall far from the Tree. I also had and continue to have a great love of flying.

Brenda my wife.......Kickers Soccer Club Queen.

*I'm on the left in this wrestling action shot:
Regional championship. I won it in overtime.*

My Uncle Menrath Nandor's daughter's (Gertrud) family:
Left to right: Gertrud's daughter Szofi, Kata the bride, Gabor who is
Gertrud's son and the groom, Gertrud Menrath, Joska Gertrud's husband.

Me in Pecs.. the city of my birth.

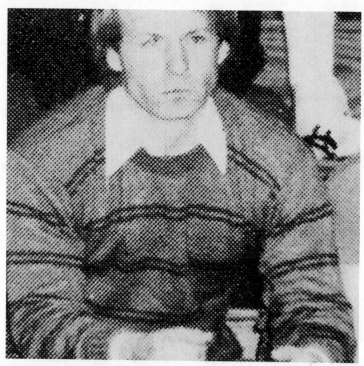

Me..as a pensive wrestling coach.

Evi my second cousin and family
L. to R. Mark Stercz, Fanni Belafi, Evi Baranyai, and Martin Stercz.

My cousin Erzsi accompanied us on our first visit back to Hungary in '68.
Left to Right: Joe my brother, Erzsi Liptak, and me.

This is the family of my cousin Gyula Suhajda. L. to R. Annie Suhajda, Mia
Fekete, Anita Suhajda, Liza Fekete, Gyula Suhajda.

Me...making a bad pass.

The Sarkodi family. Left to Right: David Sarkodi, Eszter Lovas, Oliver Sarkodi, Dora Sarkodi.

The Messerschmitt Bf 109 is a German World War II fighter aircraft.

My father...a proud owner of his first car, a '50 Ford Mercury.

Waubonsee Community College Men's Soccer team
National Qualifying Team NJCAA 2017. Tournament held in Prescott AZ.
Team was ranked among top 15 teams in the nation.